APPLIED COMPUTATIONAL MATHEMATICS IN SOCIAL SCIENCES

BY

Romulus-Catalin Damaceanu*

Faculty of Economics, "Petre Andrei" University of Iasi, Romania

eBooks End User License Agreement

CONTENTS

FOREWORD

This book explores how researchers can apply *Computational Mathematics* in *Social Sciences*. *Computational Mathematics* involves mathematical research in areas of science where computing plays a central and essential role, emphasizing algorithms, numerical methods, and symbolic methods. *Social Sciences* comprise academic disciplines concerned with the study of the social life of human groups and individuals, including the next sciences:

(i) *Anthropology* is the holistic discipline that deals with the integration of different aspects of social sciences, humanities, and human biology;

(ii) *Economics* is a social science that seeks to analyze and describe the production, distribution, and consumption of wealth;

(iii) *Education* encompasses teaching and learning of specific skills, and also something less tangible but more profound: the imparting of knowledge and well-developed wisdom;

(iv) *Geography* can be split broadly into two main subfields: human geography, and physical geography. The former focuses largely on the built environment and how space is created, viewed and managed by humans as well as the influence humans have on the space they occupy. The latter examines the natural environment and how the climate, vegetation, life, soil, water, and landforms are produced and interact;

(v) *History* is the continuous and systematic research of past events as relating to the human beings, as well as the study of all events in time, in relation to humanity;

(vi) *Law* means a rule which (unlike a rule of ethics) is capable of enforcement through institutions;

(vii) *Linguistics* is a discipline that investigates the cognitive and social aspects of human language;

(viii) *Political Science* is a discipline that deals with the theory and practice of politics, description and analysis of political systems and political behavior;

(ix) *Psychology* is an academic and applied field involving the study of human behavior and mental processes;

(x) *Social Work* is concerned with social problems, their causes, their solutions, and their human impacts;

(xi) *Sociology* is the study of society and human social action. It generally concerns itself with the social rules and processes that bind and separate people not only as individuals, but as members of associations, groups, communities, and institutions, and include the examination of the organization, and development of human social life.

All these eleven sciences are dealing with complex systems that imply an interdisciplinary research approach that combine knowledge from *Computational Mathematics* and *Social Sciences*. The problems connected with *Social Sciences* can be solved using *agent-based modeling (ABM)*. This technique uses a computational model for simulating the actions and interactions of autonomous individuals in a network, with a view to assess the effects on the system as a whole. *ABM* combines elements of game theory, complex systems, emergence, multi-agents systems and evolutionary programming. *Monte Carlo Methods* are used to introduce randomness.

The book applies an interdisciplinary approach, that combines knowledge from Applied Computational Mathematics and Social Sciences with the scope to observe, analyze and discuss the evolution of an artificial society composed by intelligent agents created in the frame of NetLogo platform.

The book is organized like this:

(i) The first chapter is an introduction of the book that gives readers the essential information regarding the two major fields approached by the book: *Applied Computational Mathematics* and *Social Sciences*;

(ii) The second chapter will describe *the multi agent-based computational model* of the artificial society that will be constructed using knowledge from the next Social Sciences: *Anthropology, Economics, Education, Geography, History, Law, Linguistics, Political Science, Psychology, Social Work,* and *Sociology*;

(iii) The third chapter will describe the implementation in NetLogo of the multi agent-based model described in the second chapter;

(iv) The fourth chapter will use the computational model implemented in the third chapter for a set of computational experiments using NetLogo;

(v) The last chapter will present the conclusions of the computational experiments done in the fourth chapter.

Alexandru Trifu

Faculty of Economics
"Petre Andrei" University of Iasi
2010

PREFACE

The topics approached by this book have received significant attention in recent years because social researchers can apply new tools in order to investigate social reality. This book presents some latest and representative developments of Applied Computational Mathematics in Social Sciences. It focuses on some major and important problems in *agent-based modeling* (*ABM*) used in Social Sciences and provide comprehensive survey of *a multi agent-based computational model* of an artificial society implemented in NetLogo, a freeware platform available on Internet.

The book consists of five chapters. Chapter 1 is the introduction of the book that gives the essential information to the readers regarding the two major fields approached by the book: *Applied Computational Mathematics* and *Social Sciences*. Chapter 2 describes *the multi agent-based computational model* of the artificial society constructed by using knowledge from the next Social Sciences: *Anthropology, Economics, Education, Geography, History, Law, Linguistics, Political Science, Psychology, Social Work,* and *Sociology*. Chapter 3 describes the implementation in NetLogo of the multi agent-based model described in the second chapter. Chapter 4 uses the computational model implemented in the third chapter for a set of computational experiments using NetLogo. Chapter 5 presents the conclusions of the computational experiments done in the fourth chapter.

The primary target audiences of this book are those who are interested in using Computational Mathematics in Social Sciences. Typically, they include scholars, researchers, developers and postgraduate students. This book could be a useful reference for university courses in both fields of Applied Computational Mathematics and Social Sciences.

CHAPTER 1

INTRODUCTION

Abstract: In this chapter, we offer the essential information to our readers regarding the two major fields approached by the book: *Applied Computational Mathematics* and *Social Sciences*. The first field emphasizes algorithms, numerical methods, and symbolic methods. The development of this field created new scientific disciplines like: Computational Biology, Computational Chemistry, Computational Economics, Computational Electrodynamics, Computational Finance, Computational Fluid Dynamics, Computational Geophysics, Computational Mechanics, Computational Physics, and Computational Statistics. On the other hand, Social Sciences comprise academic disciplines concerned with the study of the social life of human groups and individuals, and are dealing with complex systems that imply an interdisciplinary research approach, that combines knowledge from Computational Mathematics and Social Sciences. The problems connected with Social Sciences can be solved by using *agent-based modeling* (*ABM*). This technique uses a computational model for simulating the actions and interactions of autonomous individuals in a network, with a view to study the effects on the system as a whole. In order to create and implement a multi-agent computational model, you need a software platform. We are going to use NetLogo software platform. NetLogo uses three types of agents A: turtles T_i, patches P_{xy} and observer O. The main construction blocks of any agent-based computational model are the next: the set of agents (A), the initializations (I), and the simulation specifications (R).

This book applies an interdisciplinary approach that combines knowledge from Applied Computational Mathematics and Social Sciences with the scope to observe, analyze and discuss the evolution of an artificial society composed by intelligent agents created in the frame of NetLogo platform. In the last years, a new scientific approach developed in the study of complex systems in a unified framework. This approach is strongly rooted in the advances that have been made in diverse scientific fields. The goal of this new approach is to understand the properties of complex systems. Despite the great complexity and variety of this kind of systems, there are certain universal laws and phenomena that are essential to our inquiry and understanding. Thus, all scientific research is based, to a greater or lesser degree, on the existence of universality, which manifests itself in diverse ways.

If we try to define the word "complex" then we can say that this is consisting of interconnected parts. Now, we can say that simple systems are also formed out of parts. To explain the difference between simple and complex systems, the term "interconnected" is essential. In order to understand the behavior of a complex system, we must understand not only the behavior of the parts but how they act together to form the behavior of the whole system. Because we cannot describe the whole system without describing each part, and because each part must be described in relation to other parts, the complex systems are difficult to understand and study. This is the main reason of a label attached to this type of systems: "not easy to understand or analyze".

For many years, professional specialization has led to a progressive isolation of individual scientific disciplines. This isolation can be transformed in cooperation between different scientific fields by adapting the tools developed by a certain discipline to a more general use by recognizing their universal applicability. Hence is the motivation for cross-disciplinary scientific research in the study of complex systems.

Applied Computational Mathematics involves mathematical research in areas of science where computing plays a central and essential role, emphasizing algorithms, numerical methods, and symbolic methods. Computational mathematics emerged as a distinct part of applied mathematics by early 1950s. Currently, Applied Computational Mathematics is the field of study concerned with constructing mathematical models and numerical solution techniques by using computers in order to analyze and solve scientific, social scientific and engineering problems. In practical use, it is typically the application of computer simulation and other forms of computation to problems in various scientific disciplines. Scientists specialized in Applied Computational Mathematics develop computer programs, application software, that model systems being studied and run these programs with various sets of input parameters. Numerical analysis is an important technique used in Applied Computational Mathematics.

The development of Applied Computational Mathematics created new scientific fields like:

(i)   **Computational Biology** is a science that applies the techniques of Computer Science, Applied Mathematics, and Statistics to solve the specific problems of Biology;

Romulus-Catalin Damaceanu (Ed)

(ii) Computational Chemistry uses computers for solving chemical problems by using the results of theoretical chemistry, incorporated into computer programs used to calculate the structures and properties of molecules and solids. In some cases, this approach may predict unobserved chemical phenomena;

(iii) **Computational Economics** includes fields like Agent-based Computational Modeling, Computational Econometrics and Statistics, Computational Finance, Computational Modeling of Dynamic Macroeconomic Systems, etc., that explore the intersections of Economics with Computation Techniques;

(iv) **Computational Electrodynamics** can be defined as the process of modeling the interaction of electromagnetic fields with physical objects and the environment;

(v) **Computational Finance** is an inter-disciplinary field which combines knowledge from Mathematical Finance, Numerical Methods and Computer Simulations to make trading, hedging, and investment decisions, as well as facilitating the risk management of those decisions. The purpose is to precisely determine the financial risk of certain financial instruments;

(vi) **Computational Fluid Dynamics** uses numerical methods and algorithms to solve and analyze problems that involve fluid flows. Computers perform the millions of calculations required to simulate the interaction of fluids and gases with the complex surfaces used in engineering;

(vii) **Computational Geophysics** uses numerical computations to analyze geophysical data obtained by observations. Computing plays a major role due to the size and complexity of the geophysical data to be processed. The main computing demanding tasks are: 3D images building of the earth surface; Modeling of complex media, etc;

(viii) **Computational Mechanics** uses computational methods to study phenomena of Mechanics;

(ix) **Computational Physics** implements numerical algorithms to solve problems in Physics for which a quantitative theory already exists. This science is a branch between theoretical and experimental physics;

(x) **Computational statistics** is an inter-disciplinary science that entails Statistics, Computer science and Numerical Analysis. We can consider as the area of computational science (or scientific computing) specific to the mathematical science of Statistics.

On the other hand, **Social Sciences** comprise academic disciplines concerned with the study of the social life of human groups and individuals, including the next sciences:

(i) **Anthropology** is the science that deals with the integration of different aspects of the Social Sciences, Humanities, and Human Biology;

(ii) **Economics** is a social science that analyzes and describes the production, distribution, and consumption of wealth;

(iii) **Education** studies teaching and learning of specific skills, and the imparting of knowledge and well-developed wisdom;

(iv) **Geography** has two main fields: **Human Geography** and **Physical Geography**. The first studies and analyses the built environment and how space is created, viewed and managed by humans as well as the influence of humans on the space they occupy. The second examines the natural environment and how the climate, vegetation and life, soil, water and, landforms are produced and interact;

(v) **History** can be defined as the continuous, systematic and narrative research of past events of the human species; as well as the study of all events in time, connected to the humanity;

(vi) **Law** means a rule which (unlike a rule of ethics) is capable of enforcement through institutions;

(vii) **Linguistics** investigates the cognitive and social aspects of human language;

(viii) **Political Science** studies the theory and practice of politics, analyses the political systems, and the political behavior;

(ix) **Psychology** is involved in the study of human behavior and mental processes;

(x) **Social Work** deals with social problems, their causes, their solutions and their impacts on humans;

(xi) **Sociology** analyses the society and the human social action. This science studies the social rules and the processes that bind and separate people not only as individuals, but as members of associations, groups, communities, and institutions, and includes the study of the organization, and development of human social life.

All these eleven sciences are dealing with complex systems that imply an interdisciplinary research approach that combine knowledge from **Computational Mathematics** and **Social Sciences**. The problems connected with **Social Sciences** can be solved using *agent-based modeling (ABM)*. This technique uses a computational model for simulating the actions and interactions of autonomous individuals in a network, with a view to assessing the effects on the system as a whole. *ABM* combines elements of game theory, complex systems, emergence, multi-agents systems and evolutionary programming. *Monte Carlo Methods* are used to introduce randomness. The models simulate the simultaneous operations of multiple agents, in an attempt to re-create and predict the actions of complex phenomena. The process is one of emergence from the lower (micro) level of systems to a higher (macro) level. The individual agents are presumed to be acting in what they perceive as their own interests, such as reproduction, economic benefit, or social status, and their knowledge is limited.

Agent-based simulations use generative computational approaches for analyzing "complex social systems." Examples of such systems include the population in a geographical area, and the brokers in a stock market. The *agents* in these two systems are individuals and stock brokers, respectively. These agents interact in the sense that individuals come into contact with other individuals and brokers trade shares. This type of systems is called *multi-agent social systems*. In addition, we can consider these systems to be "complex" if the number of agents is large, if the agent interactions are involved, and if the agents are heterogeneous.

Under these assumptions, we can define a complex social system as a large set of heterogeneous social agents interacting with each other.

An *agent-based simulation* of a complex social system is a computer program that creates a model of the social system to be studied by incorporating the social agents and their rules of interaction. This simulation can be deterministic (i.e., the evolution of agents is governed by deterministic rules) or stochastic (if these rules are stochastic).

Two common methods, namely *discrete event simulation* and *time-stepped simulation*, are often used to implement agent-based models [1-3]. If we use discrete event simulation method, for each event occurred in the system we assign a time of occurrence. The set of events is sorted in increasing order in function of their times of occurrence. The simulation clock is increased with a certain value when all the events of the respective time have been executed. This type of simulation is used by queuing systems [4]. The second type of simulation method (the time-stepped method) increases the value of simulation clock with a constant value. In function on the nature of the system that is modeled, the researcher can select one of these two available methods taking into account the computational speed [5]. In our case, we selected the second method of simulation.

The Agent-based Artificial Society (*AAS*) described in Chapter 2 of this book is a grouping of individual artificial entities called agents (*A*) characterized by common interests that may have distinctive culture and institutions, and are part of an economic, social and industrial infrastructure. In order to create and implement a multi-agent artificial society, you need a software platform. A simple and accessible platform for creating agent-based artificial societies is NetLogo [6-7]. A similar platform, StarLogo, has also been released with similar functionality - see http://education.mit.edu/starlogo-tng/. For Java programmers, we have Ascape - see http://ascape.sourceforge.net/. Another software package is LSD that has user-friend interface and can be used with very good results - see http://www.business.aau.dk/lsd/ [8].

We are going to use NetLogo software platform. NetLogo uses three types of agents *A*: turtles T_i, patches P_{xy} and observer *O* – see (Fig. **1**) [7]. Turtles T_i are agents that are moving inside the world, where $i \in \{0,1,2,3,...\}$ is the identification number of the turtle. The world is a bi-dimensional lattice composed by patches P_{xy}, where $x, y \in R$ are the coordinates of patches. The observer *O* does not have a specific location - we can imagine it like an entity that observes the world composed by turtles and patches. The active elements of the agent-based computational models are the set of algorithms *ALG* because these are working with the other types of elements: parameters, variables and agents (observer *O*, turtles T_i and patches P_{xy}). If the computational model did not have any computational algorithm then it will not run. Under these circumstances, all the agent-based computational models implemented using NetLogo have at least one observer algorithm. If this observer algorithm does not exist than the computational models will not run because this declares all the parameters and initial variables, setup the patches and turtles, and calls the patch-own ($ALG(P_{xy})$) and turtle-own algorithms ($ALG(T_i)$) – see (Fig. **2**).

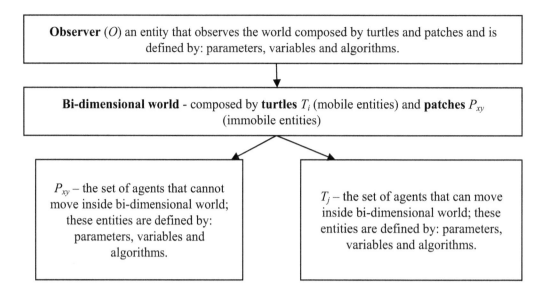

Figure 1: The agents of NetLogo

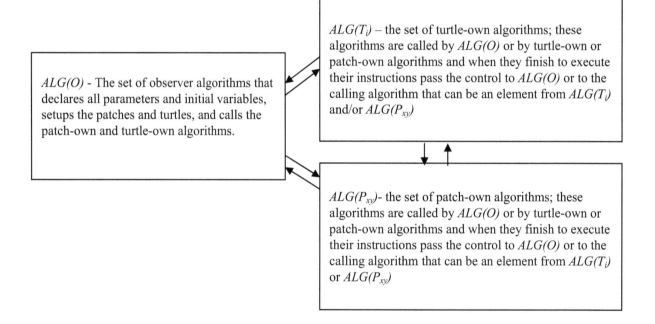

Figure 2: The set of algorithms ALG

The development of theory and applications of agent-based computational models determined in the last years a real revolution regarding the modeling of complex social systems [9-21]. The history of the agent based models can be traced back to the Von Neumann machine, a theoretical machine capable of reproduction [22]. The concept was improved by Stanislaw Ulam. Another improvement was brought by John Conway. He constructed the well-known Game of Life [23]. The birth of agent based modeling in social sciences was primarily brought by Craig Reynolds [24]. Joshua M. Epstein and Robert Axtell developed the first large scale agent-based model, the Sugarscape, to simulate and explore the role of social phenomenon such as seasonal migrations, pollution, sexual reproduction, combat, and transmission of disease and even culture [12]. More recently, Ron Sun developed methods for cognitive social simulation [25].

The main construction blocks of any agent-based computational model are the next: the set of agents (A), the initializations (I) and simulation specifications (R) – see (Fig. **3**).

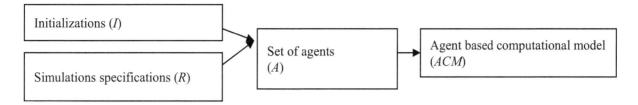

Figure 3: The elements of *ACM*

The set of agents *A* contain all *agents* defined as artificial entities that encapsulate the next elements: parameters, variables, and algorithms. *Parameters* have numerical values that do not modify on the entire period of simulation. Normally, parameters are initialized before simulation. However, in some situations they can be changed during the simulation. *Variables* are labels that have a number of values during the simulation. *Algorithms* are a finite list of well-defined instructions for accomplishing some task that, given an initial state, will proceed through a well-defined series of successive states, possibly eventually terminating in an end-state. The concept of an algorithm originated as a means of recording procedures for solving mathematical problems such as finding the common divisor of two numbers. Algorithms are essential to the way computers process information, because a computer program is essentially an algorithm that tells the computer what specific steps to perform (in what specific order) in order to carry out a specified task.

Initializations *I* are a set of identities that have in left side the variable or parameter name and in the right side the associated value.

The simulation specifications *R* are a set of identities that have in the left side the control parameter name and in the right side the associated value.

Under these circumstances an agent-based computational model (*ACM*) can be defined as a list of three arguments: the set of agents (*A*), the initializations (*I*) and simulation specifications (*R*). Shortly, *ACM = (A, I, R)*.

The study of *ACM* is concerned with the development and analysis of sophisticated artificial intelligence problem solving for both single-agent and multiple-agent systems. These systems are also referred to as "self-organized systems" as they tend to find the best solution for their problems "without intervention" [25].

In (Fig. **4**), we describe the five implementation cycles of ACM:

-    Cycle (1): modification of simulation specifications;
-    Cycle (2): modification of parameters;
-    Cycle (3): modification of initial values of variables;
-    Cycle (4): modification of algorithms;
-    Cycle (5): development of new agents.

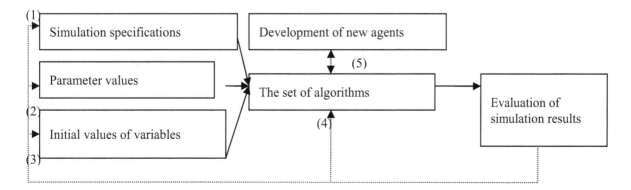

Figure 4: The five implementation cycles of ACM

Cycle (1) is the most frequent used. In this case, the researcher uses a previous created ACM or a new one in an incipient form, modifies the simulation specifications, runs the model, evaluates the simulation results and in function of these results takes the decision to apply one of the five available cycles.

Cycle (2) starts by changing the parameter values, running ACM, evaluation of results and in function of outcomes the researches apply one of the five cycles.

Cycle (3) modifies the initial values of variables, runs ACM, evaluates the results and in function of these the researcher takes the decision to apply one of the five cycles.

Cycle (4) modify the set of algorithms, runs the model and in function of results evaluation the researcher apply one of the five cycles.

Cycle (5) develop new agents, run the model and in function of results the researcher takes the decision to apply one of five available cycles. This cycle usually creates new ACM.

Implementation of ACM is different in the case of social sciences if we compare with real sciences such as Physics, Biology, Chemistry, etc. On this issue, Cohen and Cyert state the next: "In social science, generally, the situation is ... [that] the behavior of the total system can be observed. The problem is to derive a set of component relations which will lead to a total system exibiting the observed characteristics of behavior. The procedure is to construct a model which specifies the behavior of the components, and then analyze the model to determine whether or not the behavior of the model corresponds with the observed behavior of the total system" [26]. Under these circumstances, the few quantitative measurements recorded are influenced by non-mechanic phenomena such as human behavior and the reproduction of numerical series is very difficult. With other words, in the field of social sciences, the quantitative data are so insufficient and can be determined by a lot of processes that act in parallel that these data cannot be used to confirm or infirm a certain theory.

However, it is a well-known fact that many scientists use ACM in social sciences. The purpose of this kind of research is to see what is going to happen if certain hypotheses are fulfilled, with other words to control if a set of hypotheses are producing or not an expected set of results. In many cases, the expected results are not obtained and in this case the researcher may find a new theory in order to find the cause of obtained data.

We must note those social sciences scientists that implement ACM for their research do not need to have a diploma in Computer Sciences. The necessary knowledge to write the source code for ACM implementation are minimal and are strongly connected with the functioning mechanism of ACM and less connected with knowing a certain programming language. If we take into consideration that Computer Sciences are included in most of Social Sciences Curricula, then these skills are obtained during the training process of almost any social sciences researcher.

Even if the necessary knowledge of ACM implementation is minimal, we must not forget that this job is still difficult and imply certain technical aspects that are sometimes not easy to deal with. Under these circumstances, we must follow a certain working methodology that is based on the next fundamental principles:

(i)   Implement just few code lines with minimal scientific meaning;

(ii) Add new lines only when the already added lines are extensively tested;

(iii) Start from the premise that any code line may contain an error.

The application of these principles is mandatory because the programming errors recognized by computer are only a small part of all possible errors. For example, the theoretical errors are very difficult to discover and correct. These are code lines that are correctly executed by computer but do not express the theoretical concepts of the researcher. To identify these errors, it is necessary not only to study in detail the code lines but to analyze the entire set of obtained data produced by ACM implementation from the perspective of abstract theoretical concepts implemented by ACM.

REFERENCES

[1]   Bagrodia RL. Parallel languages for discrete-event simulation models. IEEE Computational Science and Engineering 1998; 5: 27–38.
[2]   Jefferson DR. Virtual time, ACM Transactions on Programming Languages and Systems 1985; 7: 404–25.
[3]   Nance RE. A history of discrete event simulation programming languages. ACM SIGPLAN Notices 1993; 28: 149–75.
[4]   Misra J. Distributed discrete-event simulation, ACM Computing Surveys 1986; 18: 39–65.
[5]   Guo Y, Gong W, Towsley D. Time-stepped hybrid simulation (tshs) for large scale networks. In INFOCOM 2000. Nineteenth Annual Joint Conference of the IEEE Computer and Communications Societies. Proceedings. IEEE, 2000; vol. 2: 441–50.

[6]   Damaceanu RC. An agent-based computational study of wealth distribution in function of resource growth interval using NetLogo. Applied Mathematics and Computation 2008; 201(1): 371-77.

[7]   Wilensky U. NetLogo. http://ccl.northwestern.edu/netlogo/. Center for Connected Learning and Computer-Based Modeling. Evanston, IL: Northwestern University; 1999.

[8]   Damaceanu RC. Implementation of simulation model of world economy using LSD. Applied Mathematics and Computation 2007; 189: 1011-24.

[9]   Arthur WB, Durlauf SN, Lane DA (Eds.). The economy as an evolving complex system II. in the Sciences of Complexity, Reading, Proceedings Vol. XXVII. MA: Addison-Wesley; 1997.

[10]   Batten D. Discovering artificial economics: How Agents Learn and Economies Evolve. CO Boulder: Westview Press; 2000

[11]   Day R, Chen P. Nonlinear Dynamics and Evolutionary Economics. Oxford, UK: Oxford University Press; 1993.

[12]   Epstein JM, Axtell R. Growing Artificial Societies: Social Science from the Bottom Up. Cambridge, MA: MIT Press; 1996.

[13]   Holland J. Adaptation in Natural and Artificial Systems: An Introductory Analysis with Applications to Biology, Control, and Artificial Intelligence. Cambridge, MA: The MIT Press; 1992.

[14]   Krugman P. The self-organizing economy. Cambridge, MA: Blackwell Publishers; 1996

[15]   Sargent T. Bounded Rationality in Macroeconomics. Oxford, UK: The Arne Ryde Memorial Lectures, Clarendon Press; 1993.

[16]   Young HP. Individual Strategy and Social Structure. Princeton, NJ: Princeton University Press; 1998.

[17]   Gorobets A, Nooteboom B. Adaptive Build-up and Breakdown of Trust: An Agent Based Computational Approach. Journal of Management and Governance 2006; 10: 277-306.

[18]   Chen SH. Computational Intelligence in Agent-Based Computational Economics. Studies in Computational Intelligence (SCI) 2008; 115: 517–594.

[19]   Dawid H, Reimann M. Evaluating Market Attractiveness: Individual Incentives Versus Industry Profitability. Computational Economics 2005; 24:321-55.

[20]   Marks RE. Validating Simulation Models: A General Framework and Four Applied Examples. Computational Economics 2007; 30: 265-290.

[21]   Gilbert N, Terna P. How to build and use agent-based models in social science. Mind & Society 2000; 1: 57-72.

[22]   Neumann J. Theory of Self-Reproducing Automata. Urbana and London: University of Illinois Press; 1966.

[23]   Gardner M. Mathematical Games - The fantastic combinations of John Conway's new solitaire game "life". Scientific American 1970; 223: 120-23.

[24]   Reynolds C. Flocks, herds and schools: A distributed behavioral model. Proceedings of the 14th annual conference on Computer graphics and interactive techniques. 1987; 25-34.

[25]   Sun R. Cognition and Multi-Agent Interaction: From Cognitive Modeling to Social Simulation. Cambridge University Press; 2006.

[26]   Cohen K, Cyert R. Computer models in dynamic economics, Quarterly Journal of Economics 1961; 75(1): 112-27.

CHAPTER 2

The Description of the Agent-Based Artificial Society (AAS)

Abstract: The status of linearity of social sciences was attacked by two major approaches developed inside Mathematics: the catastrophe theory and chaos theory. Under these conditions, the social sciences are in natural continual evolution distinguished in 5 stages: (i) The verbal description of the subject and the logic of problem, (ii) The formal identification of problem and quantification of mathematical relations, (iii) Taking into account the dynamic aspects of mathematical model under the form of linear dynamic models, (iv) The reconsideration of the basic scientific principles, including some nonlinear aspects in dynamic models, (v) The development of new complete nonlinear dynamic models able to explain all the possible phenomena verbally described in the first stage. A theory of nonlinear dynamics of fifth stage does not exist now. Generally speaking, an Agent-based Artificial Society (*AAS*) is a grouping of individual artificial entities called agents (*A*) characterized by common interests that may have distinctive culture and institutions, and that are the part of an economic, social, and industrial infrastructure. This type of society is the result of interdisciplinary scientific efforts made by people from fields, such as Applied Computational Mathematics and Social Sciences. The basic elements of the *AAS* are agents *A* that encapsulates parameters, variables and algorithms. The other basic element of the *AAS* is the Artificial Social Group (*ASG*) defined as a collection of agents, who share certain characteristics, interact with one another, accept expectations and obligations as members of the same social group, and share a common identity.

The outstanding development of computational tools in the last 30 years had a huge impact on all sciences. In social sciences, the purpose of simulation tools was at the beginning purely theoretical. This approach is motivated by the fact that since the middle of 20th century, equilibrium oriented approach was the mainstream developed to a highly sophisticated level by neoclassical Economics. Thus, in the frame of mainstream Economics, the theory is focused on static equilibrium (the dynamic equilibrium being approached as instant passing from one state of equilibrium to another as in Newton's Mechanics. The notion of equilibrium is used in many sciences as Mechanics, Thermodynamics, Biology, Economics, etc. to designate the state of a system that, in the absence of any external perturbation, can be maintained for an unlimited period of time. Thus, in Social Sciences, the equilibrium can be defined according to this approach as the state when all social agents are interested in not changing this state by using the available means of everyone. The standard general equilibrium model, conceived by Walras [1] at the end of 19th century and formalized by Arrow and Debreu [2], supposes the continuity at the base of economic agents behavior and technological changes, that combined with the convexity, generates the continual curves of offer and demand, and the existence of equilibrium. The associated linear models generated continual dynamics. For this type of models, it is very hard to obtain an algebraic formal solution. For example, even for the simplest model of world economy with two production factors and two products that uses Cobb-Douglass functions, the formal solution is very hard to find [3]. To find a numeric solution for this simplified model you must use computer programs. The development of numeric algorithms, that can be used to find the equilibrium solution for such simplified models, started 20 years ago [4].

As consequence, at the base of social theories used in our days, there are linear models including those that can be transformed in linear forms using Mathematics. This idealization of social reality is explainable up to a point. But in our days, taking into account the general development of all sciences, this approach can not be maintained in our opinion.

In a progressive manner, this status of linearity of social sciences was attacked by many scientists but it was not collapsed by these. The main pressures are coming outside Social Sciences from Mathematics and Physics. Generally, two major approaches were developed inside Mathematics. They are axed on the idea of bifurcation and breaking of equilibrium in critical points, on one hand, and on idea of that some functional relations considered to be linear are in fact nonlinear, on other hand. These approaches are different in function of concentration on large scale discontinuity (catastrophe theory), or small scale discontinuity (chaos theory). The theory of catastrophe was developed in the first stage as a special case of bifurcation theory of Henry Poincare by Rene Thom [5] and Christopher Zeeman [6]. The bases of chaos theory were put by Edward Lorenz [7], Steve Smale [8] and Benoit Mandelbrot [9-10]. These two theories were integrated by Herman Haken [11-12] by creating the synergetic theory in close relation with Ilya Prigogine's theory of dissipative structures [13].

Under these conditions, the social sciences are in natural continual evolution. Regarding this aspect, West has distinguished 5 stages of scientific progress [14]:

(i)   The verbal description of the subject and the logic of problem;

(ii)   The formal identification of problem and quantification of mathematical relations;

(iii) Taking into account the dynamic aspects of mathematical model under the form of linear dynamic models;

(iv) The reconsideration of the basic scientific principles by including some nonlinear aspects in dynamic models;

(v) The development of new complete nonlinear dynamic models able to explain all the possible phenomena verbally described in the first stage.

For example, if we take one of Social Sciences such as Economics then it is relatively easy to classify the economists in these five stages enumerated above. Thus, classical authors like Smith, Ricardo, and Malthus [15-17] can be included in the first stage. The second stage is occupied by neoclassical economists like Marshall [18], Walras [1], and Pareto [19]. The sophisticated mathematical literature on the existence of equilibriums and their stability in the frame of general equilibrium scheme of such authors like Arrow and Debreu [2] can be assigned to the third stage. The literature of agent-based computational economics and evolutionary economics can be included in the fourth stage [20-31]. An economic theory of nonlinear dynamics of fifth stage does not exist now.

Generally speaking, an Agent-based Artificial Society (*AAS*) is a grouping of individual artificial entities called agents (*A*) characterized by common interests that may have distinctive culture and institutions, and, that are part of an economic, social and industrial infrastructure. *AAS* is used for computer simulation in social analysis. This concept has been widely accepted as a method characterized by the use of computer programs and computer simulations which include agent based models. This type of society is the result of interdisciplinary scientific efforts done by people from fields such as Applied Computational Mathematics and Social Sciences.

The basic elements of the *AAS* are agents *A*. As we have already defined in Chapter 1, these encapsulate parameters, variables and algorithms. The other basic element of the *AAS* is the Artificial Social Group (*ASG*) defined as a collection of agents who share certain characteristics, interact with one another, accept expectations and obligations as members of the same social group, and share a common identity. Characteristics that members in the group may share include interests, values, ethnic/linguistic background, and kinship ties.

ASG can be of two types: primary *ASG* and secondary *ASG*. Primary *ASG* consist of small groups with intimate, kin-based relationships: families, for example. Secondary *ASG*, in contrast to primary groups, are large groups whose relationships are formal and institutional. Some of them may last for years but some may disband after a short lifetime. The formation of primary *ASG* happens within secondary *ASG*.

Under these circumstances, any *AAS* can be described as we can see in (Fig. **1**). As we can see in this figure, an agent *A* can be included in one or more *ASG*. For example, an agent can be a member of one primary *ASG*, i.e. a family and, in addition, the same agent can be member of one secondary *ASG*, i.e. a country.

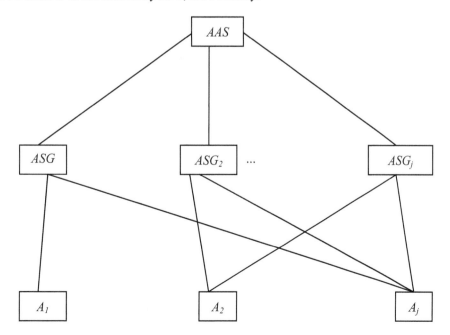

Figure 1: The structure of Agent-based Artificial Society

THE GENERAL CHARACTERISTICS OF AAS

An Agent-based Artificial Society has some general characteristics described below:

(i) An *AAS* is extremely complex and dynamic. The complexity of this kind of system is determined by the number of components and the connections between them, and by the particular characteristics of social phenomena and processes. A social phenomenon or process is the transition of *AAS* from one state to another. The state of AAS is identified with a set of parameters and variables that describes the entire characteristics of *AAS*;

(ii) An *AAS* is extremely profound and, in the same time, is described by a different degree of intensity for informational and material connections of its elements. It is important to note that every element of *AAS* can interact with other elements but not with the entire set of elements. Regarding the intensity of connections between the elements, this one is very heterogeneous. The profundity and intensity of connections between *AAS* elements are criteria for identifications of subsystems of *AAS*. From this point of view, by *AAS* subsystem we understand a set of elements with such intense connections that exceed the intensity of other connections or interactions with the surrounding environment. The informational and material flows between elements of *AAS* can put in direct connection two or more elements of *AAS* or *AAS* subsystems or in intermediate connection using some intermediary elements. The social connections between elements of *AAS* can be on horizontal or on vertical. The entire system can be represented under the form of ordered string of elements, every of these elements being independent in comparison with other elements on the same horizontal. The elements of the same horizontal are components in comparison with the subsystem located on the upper level on vertical;

(iii) Another characteristic of *AAS* is given by the property of its elements to control one or more parameters and variables. The changing operated by an element of *AAS* over its control parameter(s) or variable(s) determine an influence over "neighborhood", but the intensity of reaction is very heterogeneous. Under these circumstances, it is very difficult to foresee all the consequences of such changing;

(iv) *AAS* has as fundamental characteristic the combination of deterministic and stochastic features of connections between its elements;

(v) *AAS* and its subsystems are included in the class of systems with self organizing that have the capacity to modify their internal structure. Thus, *AAS* subsystems located on the same level can unify or split and this modify the internal organization of the subsystems located on the upper level;

(vi) A fundamental characteristic of *AAS* and its subsystems is the capacity to adapt in order to survive under the assumption that the information is incomplete or imperfect. In adaptation processes, some subsystems of *AAS* have the capacity to modify the external environment. With other words, these elements can adapt to external conditions in order to fulfill their own objectives;

(vii) *AAS* subsystems are open, and they cannot be completely isolated from their surrounding environment. Under certain conditions, these systems can be in a state of dynamic equilibrium with the environment. Because of their openness, *AAS* subsystems can maintain a high level of organizing, and evolve in the sense of order and complexity.

AAS SEEN FROM THE POINT OF VIEW OF APPLIED COMPUTATIONAL MATHEMATICS

The agent-based artificial society described in this chapter is using three types of resources: water, food, and energy. This society has the next characteristics:

(i) the turtles T_i are of two types: female and male;

(ii) these turtles have a limited life expectancy determined by the parameters E_i (maximum life expectancy) and e_i (minimum life expectancy);

(iii) the patches P_{xy} are of three types: type 1 that stores a certain amount of water $w_{xy} \geq 0$, type 2 that stores a certain amount of food $f_{xy} \geq 0$, and type 3 that stores a certain amount of energy $e_{xy} \geq 0$;

(iv) a male and female turtle can create a couple, and a number of children;

(v) the children can inherit the wealth of their parents;

(vi) the basic needs of every turtle are 1 unit of water, 1 unit of food, and 1 unit of energy per one year;

(vii) if these basic needs are not fulfilled then the respective turtle dies.

In (Fig. **2**), there is described the structure of *ACM* of *AAS*. In (Table **1**), there are described the parameters, variables, and algorithms of observer *O*, turtles T_i and patches P_{xy}.

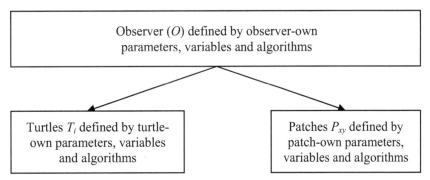

Figure 2: The structure of ACM of AAS

Table 1: The parameters, variables and algorithms of observer *O*, turtles T_i and patches P_{xy}

Label	Type	Agent	Description
t	Variable	Observer O	the number of years
s	Parameter	Observer O	the seed of pseudo random number generator, $s \in \{-2,-1,0,1,2\}$
z	Parameter	Observer O	has two possible values 0 for nonrenewable resources and 1 for renewable resources
f	Parameter	Observer O	the initial number of females, $f=5$
m	Parameter	Observer O	the initial number of males, $m=5$
n_t	Variable	Observer O	the number of turtles
f_t	Variable	Observer O	the number of females
m_t	Variable	Observer O	the number of males
v	Parameter	Observer O	the maximum possible vision of turtles, $v=15$
E	Parameter	Observer O	maximum life expectancy, $E=80$
e	Parameter	Observer O	minimum life expectancy, $e=30$
A	Parameter	Observer O	the age when the sexual life starts, $A=20$
r	Parameter	Observer O	the value of resources growth interval, $r \in \{1,2,3,4,5,6,7,8,9,10\}$
w_t	Variable	Observer O	mean wealth in water
f_t	Variable	Observer O	mean wealth in food
e_t	Variable	Observer O	mean wealth in energy
W_t	Variable	Observer O	mean global wealth
v^l_t	Variable	Observer O	the average vision for low class
v^m_t	Variable	Observer O	the average vision for medium class
v^h_t	Variable	Observer O	the average vision for high class
n^l_t	Variable	Observer O	the number of turtles from low class
n^m_t	Variable	Observer O	the number of turtles from medium class
n^h_t	Variable	Observer O	the number of turtles from high class
W^l_t	Variable	Observer O	the average wealth for low class
W^m_t	Variable	Observer O	the average wealth for medium class
W^h_t	Variable	Observer O	the average wealth for high class
InitPVA	Algorithm	Observer O	Initialization of parameters, variables and algorithms
Setup	Algorithm	Observer O	Setup of computer simulation
Go	Algorithm	Observer O	Start of computer simulation
i	Parameter	Turtles T_i	the identification number of the turtle, $i \in \{0,1,2,...,n_t-1\}$

Table 1: cont....

x^i_t	Variable	Turtles T_i	the current x coordinate of the turtle
y^i_t	Variable	Turtles T_i	the current y coordinate of the turtle
h^i_t	Variable	Turtles T_i	the direction the turtle is facing; This is a number greater than or equal to 0 and less than 360
f_i	Parameter	Turtles T_i	the identification number of mother, $f_i \in \{0,1,2,...,n_t\text{-}1\}$
m_i	Parameter	Turtles T_i	the identification number of father, $m_i \in \{0,1,2,...,n_t\text{-}1\}$
t_i	Variable	Turtles T_i	the age of the turtle
E_i	Parameter	Turtles T_i	maximum age that a turtle can reach, $E_i \in [e,E] \cap N$
v_i	Parameter	Turtles T_i	the vision of the turtle (how many patches ahead a turtle can see for harvesting), $v_i \in \{1,2,..., v\}$
s_i	Parameter	Turtles T_i	a boolean parameter that have two possible values: 0 if the turtle is female and 1 if the turtle is male
g^i_t	Variable	Turtles T_i	a boolean variable that have two possible values: 0 if the turtle is not engaged in a relation and 1 if the turtle is engaged
p^i_t	Variable	Turtles T_i	the identification number of the sexual partner, $p_i \in \{0,1,2,...,n_t\text{-}1\}$
w^i_t	Variable	Turtles T_i	the quantity of water owned
f^i_t	Variable	Turtles T_i	the quantity of food owned
e^i_t	Variable	Turtles T_i	the quantity of energy owned
W^i_t	Variable	Turtles T_i	the global wealth
n^i_t	Variable	Turtles T_i	a variable that have the next possible values: 0 if the turtle is not pregnant in a relation and 1 if the turtle is pregnant with female child and 2 if it is pregnant with male child
d^i_t	Variable	Turtles T_i	pregnancy duration
c^i_t	Variable	Turtles T_i	the social class: 1 for low, 2 for medium and 3 for high
TurtlesCreation	Algorithm	Turtles T_i	Create the initial number of turtles
FindResources	Algorithm	Turtles T_i	Used by turtles to find the available resources
FindWomen	Algorithm	Turtles T_i	Used by male turtles to find an available female sexual partner
DoSex	Algorithm	Turtles T_i	Used to simulate the sexual relation within a couple
EatDrinkWarmAgeDie	Algorithm	Turtles T_i	Used to eat, drink, warm, age, leave the wealth to the inheritors and die
Pregnancy	Algorithm	Turtles T_i	Used to simulate the pregnancy period and the born of new turtles
UpdateSocialClass	Algorithm	Turtles T_i	Used to update the social classes
InheritTurtle	Algorithm	Turtles T_i	Used to find the available inheritors of turtle Ti
CountInheritors(i)	Algorithm	Turtles T_i	Used to count the inheritors of turtle T_i
InheritOfTurtle(i,w,f,e)	Algorithm	Turtles T_i	Used to inherit the wealth of turtle Ti to its inheritors. Every inheritor will obtain w units of water, f units of food, and e units of energy
x, y	parameters	Patches P_{xy}	the cordinates of patch P_{xy}, $x,y \in [-10,10]$
p_{xy}	Parameter	Patches P_{xy}	the type of patch: 0 for food patch, 1 for water patch and 2 for energy patch
w^{xy}_t	Variable	Patches P_{xy}	the value of water resources
f^{xy}_t	Variable	Patches P_{xy}	the value of food resources
e^{xy}_t	Variable	Patches P_{xy}	the value of energy resources
PatchesCreation	Algorithm	Patches P_{xy}	Create three types of patches: food, energy and water
GrowResource	Algorithm	Patches P_{xy}	Grow the resources

As we can see in (Table **1**) the algorithms used by agents are grouped in three sets:

(i)   *ALG(O)*={InitPVA,Setup,Go};

(ii)   *ALG(P$_{xy}$)*={PatchesCreation,GrowResource};

(iii)   *ALG(T$_i$)*={TurtlesCreation,FindResources,FindWomen,DoSex,EatDrinkWarmAgeDie,Pregnancy,Update SocialClass,InheritTurtle,CountInheritors(a), InheritOfTurtle(a,b,c,d)}.

The first set *ALG(O)* consists in the observer algorithms: **InitPVA, Setup** and **Go**. These algorithms are detailed bellow:

(1) Algorithm InitPVA. (Initialization of parameters, variables and algorithms)

Step 1. Declare the next observer-own parameters and variables: t, s, z, f, m, n_t, f_t, m_t, v, E, e, A, r, w_t, f_t, e_t, W_t, v^l_t, v^m_t, v^h_t, n^l_t, n^m_t, n^h_t, W^l_t, W^m_t, W^h_t

Step 2. Declare the patch-own parameters and variables: x, y, p_{xy}, w_{xy}, f_{xy}, e_{xy}

Step 3. Declare the next turtle-own parameters and variables: i, f_i, m_i, t_i, E_i, v_i, s_i, g^i_t, p^i_t, w^i_t, f^i_t, e^i_t, W^i_t, n^i_t, d^i_t, c^t_i

Step 4. Call algorithm **Setup**

Step 5. Call algorithm **Go**

(2) Algorithm Setup. (Setup of computer simulation)

Step 1. Clear all the variables and parameters used in previous simulations

Step 2. $t:=0$, $f:=5$, $m:=5$, $v=15$, $E:=80$, $e:=30$, $A:=20$

Step 3. Set the seed of pseudo-random numbers generator to the value s

Step 4. Call algorithm **PatchesCreation**

Step 5. Call algorithm **TurtlesCreation**

Step 6. Call algorithm **UpdateSocialClass**

Step 7. $n_t:=$Count all turtles

Step 8. $f_t:=$Count all turtles with $s_i=0$

Step 9. $m_t:=$Count all turtles with $s_i=1$

Step 10. $w_t := \dfrac{\sum w^i_t}{n_t}$

Step 11. $f_t := \dfrac{\sum f^i_t}{n_t}$

Step 12. $e_t := \dfrac{\sum e^i_t}{n_t}$

Step 13. $W_t := \dfrac{\sum W^i_t}{n_t}$

Step 14. $n^l_t:=$ Count all turtles with $c^i_t=1$

Step 15. $n^m_t:=$ Count all turtles with $c^i_t=2$

Step 16. $n^h_t:=$ Count all turtles with $c^i_t=3$

Step 17. Ask all turtles with $c^i_t=1$ to set $v^l_t:=v^l_t+v_i$, $W^l_t:=W^l_t+W^i_t$

Step 18. $v^l_t := \dfrac{v^l_t}{n^l_t}$, $W^l_t := \dfrac{W^l_t}{n^l_t}$

Step 19. Ask all turtles with $c^i_t = 2$ to set $v^m_t := v^m_t + v_i$, $W^m_t := W^m_t + W^m_t$

Step 20. $v^m_t := \dfrac{v^m_t}{n^m_t}$, $W^m_t := \dfrac{W^m_t}{n^m_t}$

Step 21. Ask all turtles with $c^i_t = 3$ to set $v^h_t := v^h_t + v_i$, $W^h_t := W^h_t + W^h_t$

Step 22. $v^h_t := \dfrac{v^h_t}{n^h_t}$, $W^h_t := \dfrac{W^h_t}{n^h_t}$

(3) Algorithm Go. (Start of computer simulation)

Step 1. $t := t+1$

Step 2. If the modulo between t and r is equal with 0 then if $z=1$ call algorithm Grow Resource

Step 3. If $n_t = 0$ then stop simulation

Step 4. Ask turtles to call algorithm **FindResources** and **EatDrinkWarmAgeDie**

Step 5. Ask turtles with $s_i = 1$ and $g^i_t = 0$ and $t_i \geq A$ to call algorithm **FindWomen**

Step 6. Ask turtles with $s_i = 1$ and $g^i_t = 1$ to call algorithm **DoSex**

Step 7. Call algorithm **UpdateSocialClass**

Step 8. $n_t :=$ Count all turtles

Step 9. If $n_t \neq 0$ then:

　(i) $f_t :=$ Count all turtles with $s_i = 0$

　(ii) $m_t :=$ Count all turtles with $s_i = 1$

　(iii) $w_t := \dfrac{\sum w^i_t}{n_t}$

　(iv) $f_t := \dfrac{\sum f^i_t}{n_t}$

　(v) $e_t := \dfrac{\sum e^i_t}{n_t}$

　(vi) $W_t := \dfrac{\sum W^i_t}{n_t}$

other wise then stop simulation

Step 15. If t=1000 then stop simulation

The patches-own algorithms are detailed bellow:

(1) Algorithm PatchesCreation (Create three types of patches: food, energy and water)

Step 1. Ask patches to:

(i)   Set p_{xy} to a random value from set {0,1,2};

(ii)   if p_{xy}=0 then set f^{xy}_t:= a random value from the set {1,2,3,4,5,6,7,8,9,10}, e^{xy}_t:=0, w^{xy}_t:=0

(iv)   if p_{xy}=1 then set f^{xy}_t:=0, e^{xy}_t:= a random value from the set {1,2,3,4,5,6,7,8,9,10}, w^{xy}_t:=0

(iii) if p_{xy}=2 then set f^{xy}_t:=0, e^{xy}_t:=0, w^{xy}_t:= a random value from the set {1,2,3,4,5,6,7,8,9,10}

Step 2. If the number of patches with p_{xy}=0 is equal with zero or the number of patches with p_{xy}=1 is equal with zero or number of patches with p_{xy}=2 is equal with zero then call algorithm **PatchesCreation**

(2) Algorithm GrowResource (Grow the resources at the beginning of every year)

Step 1. Ask patches to:

(i) if p_{xy}=0 then set set f^{xy}_t:= f^{xy}_t + a random value from the set {1,2,3,4,5,6,7,8,9,10};

(ii) if p_{xy}=1 then set e^{xy}_t:= e^{xy}_t + a random value from the set {1,2,3,4,5,6,7,8,9,10}.

(iii) if p_{xy}=2 then set w^{xy}_t:= w^{xy}_t a random value from the set {1,2,3,4,5,6,7,8,9,10}

The turtles-own algorithms are detailed below:

(1) Algorithm TurtlesCreation (Create the initial number of turtles)

Step 1. Create f female turtles with the next characteristics:

t_i:=20;

s_i:=0

E_i:=1+e+Random(E-e);

v_i :=1+Random(v)

g_i:=0

p^i_t:=n/a

w^i_t:=10

f^i_t:=10

e^i_t:=10

W_i:= w^i_t + f^i_t + e^i_t

n^i_t:=0

d^i_t:=0

$x^i_{t:}=0$

$y^i_{t:}=0$

Step 2. Create m male turtles with the next characteristics:

$t_{i:}=20;$

$s_{i:}=1$

$E_{i:}=1+e+\text{Random}(E-e);$

$v_i :=1+\text{Random}(v)$

$g_{i:}=0$

$p^i_{t:}=\text{n/a}$

$w^i_{t:}=10$

$f^i_{t:}=10$

$e^i_{t:}=10$

$x^i_{t:}=0$

$y^i_{t:}=0$

$W_i:= w^i_t + f^i_t + e^i_t$

(2) Algorithm FindResources. (Used by turtles to find the available resources)

Step 1. Let be a local variable r

Step 2. $h^i_{i:}=\text{Random}(360)^1$

Step 3. Repeat for v_i times the next sequence:

- Move 1 patch forward

- $r:=f^{xy}_t / (\textbf{CountTurtlesHere}^2)$

- $f^i_{t:}= f^i_t +r$

- $f^{xy}_{t:}= f^{xy}_t -r$

- $r:=w^{xy}_t / (\textbf{CountTurtlesHere})$

- $w^i_{t:}=w^i_t +r$

- $w^{xy}_{t:}= w^{xy}_t -r$

- $r:=e^{xy}_t / (\textbf{CountTutlesHere})$

---

[1] Random(n) is a function that give a random number from the set {0,1,2,...,n} where n is a natural number strictly higher than zero.
[2] CountTurtlesHere is a function counts the turtles that are sitting on the patch where this function is called.

- $e^i_t := e^i_t + r$

- $e^{xy}_t := e^{xy}_t - r$

(3) Algorithm FindWomen. (Used by male turtles to find an available female sexual partner)

Step 1. Let be α one of female turtles with $g_i=0$ and $t_i \geq A$

Step 2. If $\alpha \neq \Phi$ then execute the next sequence:

- $g_i := 1$

- g_i: of $\alpha = 1$

- $p_i := i$ of α

- p_i of $\alpha := i$

(4) Algorithm DoSex. (Used to simulate the sexual relation within a couple)

Step 1. Let be $\beta := \text{Random}(3)$

Step 2. If $\beta = 1$ or $\beta = 2$ then let be $\gamma = i$ and ask turtles with $s_i = 0$ and $p_i = \gamma$ and $n^i_i = 0$ to set $n^i_i = \beta$ and $d^i_i = 0$

(5) Algorithm EatDrinkWarmAgeDie. (Used to eat, drink, warm, age, leave the wealth to the inheritors and die)

Step 1. If $f_i \geq 1$ then $f_i := f_t - 1$; otherwise call **InheritTurtle** and die

Step 2. If $w^i \geq 1$ then $w^i_t := w^i_t - 1$; otherwise call **InheritTurtle** and die

Step 3. If $e^i \geq 1$ then $e^i_t := e^i_t - 1$; otherwise call **InheritTurtle** and die

Step 4. $t_i := t_i + 1$

Step 5. If $s_i = 0$ and $n^i_i \neq 0$ then call algorithm **Pregnancy**

Step 6. If $t_i \geq E_i$ then execute the next sequence:

- call algorithm **InheritTurtle**

- Die

(6) Algorithm InheritTurtle. (Used to find the available inheritors of turtle Ti)

Step 1. Let be the next local variables designating the amounts of water, food and energy inherited, and, respectively, the number of inheritors:

- $i^i_w := 0$

- $i^i_f := 0$

- $i^i_e := 0$

- $i_i := \textbf{CountInheritors}(i)$

Step 2. If $i_i>0$ then set $i^i_w := {}^{w^i_w}/i_i$, $i^i_f := w^i_f/i_i$, $i^i_e := w^i_e/i_i$

Step 3. Let be a local variable $\delta:=0$

Step 4. If ii>0 then $\delta:=$ **InheritofTurtle** (i,w^i_t,f^i_t,e^i_t)

Step 5. If $\delta=0$ then execute the next sequence:

- Let be the next local variables: $a:=w^i_t$, $b:=f^i_t$, $c:=e^i_t$

- Ask one of patches with $p_{xy}=0$ to set $f^{xy}_t:=f^{xy}_t+f^i_t$

- Ask one of patches with $p_{xy}=1$ to set $w^{xy}_t:=w^{xy}_t+w^i_t$

- Ask one of patches with $p_{xy}=2$ to set $e^{xy}_t:=e^{xy}_t+e^i_t$

(7) Algorithm CountInheriters(a). (Used to count the inheritors of turtle with $i=a$)

Step 1. Let be $T:=0$ a local variable

Step 2. Ask all turtles with $f_i=a$ or $m_i=a$ to set $T:=T+1$

Step 3. Report T

(8) Algorithm InheritOfTurtle(a,b,c,d). (Used to inherit the wealth of turtle with $i=a$ to its inheritors. Every inheritor will obtain b units of water, c units of food, and d units of energy)

Step 1. Let be $R:=0$ a local variable

Step 2. Ask all turtles with $f_i=a$ or $m_i=a$ to set $w^i_t:=w^i_t+b$, $f^i_t:=f^i_t+c$, $e^i_t:=e^i_t+d$, $R:=1$

Step 3. Report R

(9) Algorithm Pregnancy. (Used to simulate the pregnancy period and the born of new turtles (female or male))

Step 1. $d^i_t:=d^i_t+1$

Step 2. If $d^i_t \geq 1$ then execute the next sequence:

- Let be a local variable $S:=n^i_t$

- $n^i_t:=0$

- $d^i_t:=0$

- Let be a local variable $F:=i$

- Let be a local variable $F_j:=f^i_t$

- Let be a local variable $E_j:=e^i_t$

- Let be a local variable $W_j:=w^i_t$

- $f^i_t:= \dfrac{9f^i_t}{10}$

- $e^i_t := \dfrac{9e^i_t}{10}$

- $w^i_t := \dfrac{9w^i_t}{10}$

- Let be a local variable $V_f := v_i$

- Let be a local variable M

- Let be a local variable $F_m := 0$

- Let be a local variable $E_m := 0$

- Let be a local variable $W_m := 0$

- Let be a local variable $V_f := 0$

- Ask all turtles with $s_i = 1$ and $p^i_t = F$ to set: $M := i$, $F_m := f^i_t$, $E_m := e^i_t$, $W_m := w^i_t$, $f^i_t := \dfrac{9f^i_t}{10}$, $e^i_t := \dfrac{9e^i_t}{10}$, $w^i_t := \dfrac{9w^i_t}{10}$, $V_f := v_i$

- If $S=1$ then create a new turtle with the next characteristics: $t_i := 0$, $s_i := 0$, $E_i := 1+e+Random(E-e)$, $v_i := 1+Random(v)$, $g_i := 0$, $p^i_t := n/a$, $w^i_t := \dfrac{W_m + W_f}{10}$, $f^i_t := \dfrac{F_m + F_f}{10}$, $e^i_t := \dfrac{E_m + E_f}{10}$, $W_i := w^i_t + f^i_t + e^i_t$, $n^i_t := 0$, $d^i_t := 0$

- If $S=2$ then create a new turtle with the next characteristics: $t_i := 0$, $s_i := 1$, $E_i := 1+e+Random(E-e)$, $v_i := 1+Random(v)$, $g_i := 0$, $p^i_t := n/a$, $w^i_t := \dfrac{W_m + W_f}{10}$, $f^i_t := \dfrac{F_m + F_f}{10}$, $e^i_t := \dfrac{E_m + E_f}{10}$, $W_i := w^i_t + f^i_t + e^i_t$, $n^i_t := 0$, $d^i_t := 0$

(10) Algorithm UpdateSocialClass. (Used to update the social classes)

Step 1. Ask all turtles to compute the global wealth: $W^i_t := w^i_t + f^i_t + e^i_t$

Step 2. Let be $W^{max}_i := MAX\, W^i_t$ [3]

Step 3. Ask all turtles:

- If $W_i \le \dfrac{W^{max}_i}{3}$ then set ci:=1

- If $\dfrac{W^{max}_i}{3} < W_i \le \dfrac{2 \cdot W^{max}_i}{3}$ then set ci:=2

- If $\dfrac{2 \cdot W^{max}_i}{3} < W_i \le W^{max}_i$ then set ci:=3

AAS SEEN FROM THE POINT OF VIEW OF SOCIAL SCIENCES

In this section, we try to analyze AAS from the point of view of *Social Sciences*. In the introductory chapter, we said that there are eleven Social Sciences. First of these sciences is *Anthropology* that integrate different aspects of Social Sciences, Humanities, and Human Biology. From the point of view of this science, AAS described in the previous section is a society composed of entities that interact, have social relations, create social groups, and try to survive in an environment exactly like biological organisms.

---

[3] *MAX(X_i)* reports the maximum number value from the set of values X_i.

The second science is *Economics* that analyze the production, distribution, and consumption of wealth. Our AAS has a production system that produce wealth, a distribution system that distribute the wealth between mobile agents, and a consumption system that uses the produced wealth to satisfy the needs of mobile agents.

The third science is *Education* that encompasses teaching and learning skills. In our case, every mobile agent has a certain vision that determines the level of skills needed to survive in the given environment.

The fourth science is *Geography*. Our AAS exists in an environment that has its own geography. The environment is a bi-dimensional lattice with a toroidal shape. Every patch of this lattice has the capacity to produce a certain amount of water, food, or energy – see (Fig. **3**), where blue patches have water resources, green patches have food resources and yellow patches have energy resources.

The fifth science is *History*. We can say that our AAS has its own history that can be analyzed on the level of the entire AAS, and on the level of AAS subsystems such as families and individual mobile agents.

The sixth science is *Law*. Our AAS has its own set of rules described below:

(i) Rule 1: Every turtle has the right to move on every patch that surrounds it;

(ii) Rule 2: Every turtle has the right to harvest the available resources on the patch where is located;

(iii) Rule 3: Every turtle has the right to inherit the wealth of its parents when these die;

(iv) Rule 4. Every turtle has the obligation to give 1/10 of its wealth to its children in the moment when this one is born;

(v) Rule 5. If a turtle has inheritors, then in the moment when die its wealth is given in equal shares to its inheritors. If the turtle has no inheritors then its wealth remains on random patches;

(vi) Rule 6. Two turtles of opposite sex can make a couple with the condition that they are not engaged in other such relation.

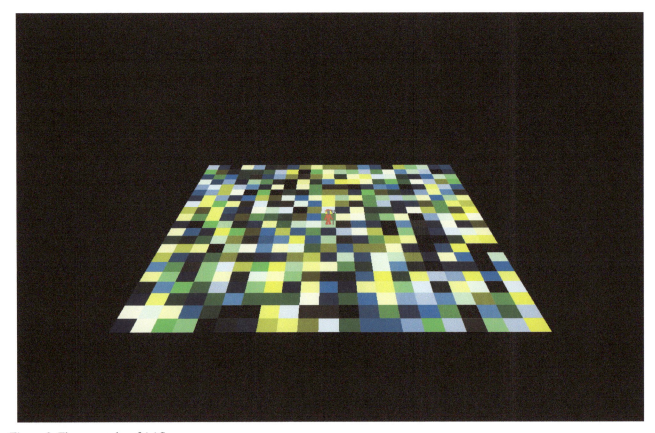

Figure 3: The geography of AAS

The seventh science is *Linguistics*. We can say that our AAS has some connection with this science if we consider that the knowledge of harvesting resources is transmitted from parents to children.

The eighth science is *Political Science*. Our AAS is too simple to consider having a political system.

The ninth science is *Psychology*. Our turtles have a peaceful behavior, they respect the law, and in such condition there are no wars.

The tenth science is *Social Work*. We can consider a social work the event when a turtle that has no inheritors leaves its wealth on random patches. In such manner, the resources accumulated are available to other turtles that have the luck to find the respective patches.

The eleventh science is *Sociology*. Our AAS has its own set of social rules and processes that exist in the frame of social groups like families.

REFERENCES

[1]   Walras L. Elements of Pure Economics. Homewood: Irwin; 1954.
[2]   Arrow KJ, Debreu G. Existence of an Equilibrium for a Competitive Economy. Econometrica 1964; 22: 265-290.
[3]   Dinwiddy CL, Teal FJ. The two-sector General Equilibrium Model: A new Approach. Oxford: Phlip Allan; 1988.
[4]   Shoven JB, Whalley J. Applying General Equilibrium. Cambridge: Cambridge University Press; 1992.
[5]   Thom R. Stabilite structurelle et Morphogenese. New York: Benjamin; 1972.
[6]   Zeeman EC. Catastrophe Theory: Selected Papers (1972-1977). Mass.: Addison-Wesley Reading; 1977.
[7]   Lorenz E. Deterministic Nonperiodic Flow, J. Atmos. Sci. 1963; 20: 130-41.
[8]   Smale S. Differential Dynamical Systems, Bulletin of the American Mathematical Society 1967; 73: 747-817.
[9]   Mandelbrot BB. The Fractal Geometry of Nature. New York: W. H. Freeman and Co.; 1982.
[10]   Mandelbrot BB. Les objets fractals: Flammarion; 1989.
[11]   Haken H. Synergetics: An Introduction. Berlin, Heidelberg: Springer; 1977.
[12]   Haken H. Advanced Synergetics. Berlin, Heidelberg: Springer; 1983.
[13]   Prigogine I. From being into Becoming: Time and Complexity in Physical Sciences. San Francisco: W. H. *Freeman* and Company; 1980.
[14]   West BJ. An Essay on the Importance of Being Nonlinear. Berlin-Heidelberg-New York: Springer; 1985.
[15]   Smith A. An inquiry into the nature and causes of the wealth of nations. New York: Cannan E. American Modern Library Series; 1937.
[16]   Ricardo D. Principles of Political Economy and Taxation, 1817. Reprinted in Sraffa P. (ed.). The works and Correspondence of David Ricardo. London: Cambridge Univeristy Press; 1951.
[17]   Malthus TR. An Essay on the Principle of Population. London: John Murray; 1826.
[18]   Marshall A. Money, Credit, and Commerce. London: MacMillan and Co., Ltd.; 1923.
[19]   Pareto V. The Mind and Society [Trattato Di Sociologia Generale]. Harcourt: Brace; 1935.
[20]   Aruka Y. Evolutionary Controversies in Economics: A New Transdisciplinary Approach. Tokyo and Berlin: Springer; 2001.
[21]   Boulding KE. What is evolutionary economics?. Journal of Evolutionary Economics 1991; 1: 9-17.
[22]   Dosi G, Orsenigo L.. Macrodynamics and microfoundations: an evolutionary perspective. In: Granstrand O. (ed.). The economics of technology. Amsterdam: North Holland; 1994: 91-124.
[23]   Fagiolo G, Dosi G., Gabriele R. Matching, Bargaining, and Wage Setting in an Evolutionary Model of Labor Market and Output Dynamics. Advances in Complex Systems 2004; 14: 157-186.
[24]   Grebel T, Pyka A, Hanusch H. An Evolutionary Approach to the Theory of the Entrepreneur. Industry and Innovation 10; Dec. 2003: 493-514.
[25]   Nelson RR, Winter SG. An Evolutionary Theory of Economic Change. Cambridge, MA: Cambridge University Press; 1982.
[26]   Nelson RR. Recent Evolutionary Theorizing About Economic Change. Journal of Economic Literature 1995; 33: 48-90.
[27]   Page SE. On Incentives and Updating in Agent Based Models. Computational Economics 1997; 10: 67-87.
[28]   Tesfatsion L. Agent-based modelling of evolutionary economic systems. IEEE Transactions on Evolutionary Computation 2001; 5: 1-6.
[29]   Tesfatsion L. Structure, Behavior, and Market Power in an Evolutionary Labor Market with Adaptive Search. Journal of Economic Dynamics and Control 2001; 25: 419-57.
[30]   Tesfatsion L. Agent-based Computational Economics: Growing Economies from the Bottom Up. Ames, Iowa, Working Paper, No.1, Iowa State University, Dept. of Economics; 2002.
[31]   Vega-Redondo F. Evolution, Games, and Economic Behavior. Oxford: Oxford University Press; 1996.

CHAPTER 3

The Implementation of the Artificial Society Using Netlogo

Abstract: An agent based model implementation is the result of three different types of scientists: the thematician, the modeler and the computer scientist. The implementation of Artificial Society using NetLogo is the process of transforming the algorithms in the procedures recognized by NetLogo. Any agent-based computational model implementation must be validated and verified. A model is valid to the extent that it provides a satisfactory range of accuracy consistent with the intended application of the model. Verification (sometimes called "internal validation") is the process of ensuring that the model performs in the manner intended by its designers and implementers. NetLogo is a software platform designed by Uri Wilensky it in the year 1999, NetLogo is used for modeling complex systems developing over time. NetLogo has a Models Library with a large collection of agent-based models that can be used and/or modified. Netlogo uses three types of agents: turtles, patches and observer. NetLogo has the next defining characteristics: (i) simplicity, (ii) transparency, (iii) gradual modeling, (iv) cross-platform, (v) extensive options of running, (vi) environment, (vii) BehaviorSpace tool, (viii) System Dynamics Modeler, (ix) speed slider, (x) powerful and flexible plotting system, (xi) HubNet module and (xii) models can be saved as applets to be embedded in web pages.

Agent-based simulation is a technique that facilitates a more direct correspondence between the entities in the target system and the parts of the model that represent them [1]. This enhances the descriptive accuracy of the modeling process, but it can also create difficulties. Under these circumstances, almost every implementation of agent-based models may contain bugs defined as code that does something different in comparison with what you expected [2]. As Axelrod underlines, you have to work hard to confirm that the implemented model was correctly programmed [3]. In addition, Axtell and Epstein state that "the robustness" of macrostructures to perturbations in individual agent performances is specific to agent-based models and makes very hard to identify bugs [4].

An agent based model implementation is the result of three different types of scientist: the thematician, the modeler and the computer scientist [5]. Thus, discovering inconsistencies in programming languages lines is in general a difficult task. Several authors [6-9] have identified the concept of ontology, defined as formal, explicit specification of a shared conceptualization [10], to be particularly promising for this purpose, especially in the domain of agent-based social simulation.

The implementation of Artificial Society using NetLogo is the process of transforming the algorithms described in Chapter 2 in procedures recognized by NetLogo. Any agent-based computational model implementation must be validated and verified. A model is valid to the extent that it provides a satisfactory range of accuracy consistent with the intended application of the model [11-12]. Thus, if the objective is to accurately represent social reality, then validation is about assessing how well the model is capturing the essence of its empirical referent. This could be measured in terms of goodness of fit to the characteristics of the model's referent [13]. Verification (sometimes called "internal validation" [14-17], [3], [5] is the process of ensuring that the model performs in the manner intended by its designers and implementers. Thus, verification is the process of looking for errors. An example of an implementation error would be the situation when the *programmer* intends to loop through the whole list of agents in the program, but he mistakenly writes the code so it only runs through a subset of them. A less trivial example of an error would be the situation where it is believed that a program is running according to the rules of real arithmetic, while the program is actually using floating-point arithmetic [18-21].

GENERAL CHARACTERISTICS OF NETLOGO

NetLogo is a software platform designed by Uri Wilensky it in the year 1999 [22]. NetLogo is in a process of development and modernization in the frame of Center for Connected Learning and Computer-Based Modeling - Northwestern University, Illinois, USA. NetLogo is written in Java language and can be run on all major platforms (Windows, Mac, Linux etc.). In addition, individual models can be run as Java applets inside web pages. NetLogo is freeware and can be downloaded from the next web address: http://ccl.northwestern.edu/netlogo/. For the moment there are available the next versions of NetLogo: NetLogo4.1beta1, NetLogo4.0.4, NetLogo3DPreview5, NetLogo 3.1.5, NetLogo 3.0.2, NetLogo2.1, NetLogo2.0.2, and NetLogo1.3.1 – see (Fig. **1**). As the site of NetLogo advices us, the right choice for the moment is NetLogo 4.0.4 and I used this version for implementing the artificial society described in Chapter 2 of this book. The newest version is NetLogo4.1beta1 but his version may contain some bugs and for this reason I did not used for this book.

NetLogo is used for modeling complex systems developing over time. You can give instructions to hundreds or thousands of agents operating concurrently. This makes it possible to explore the connection between the micro-level behavior of individuals and the macro-level patterns that result from the interactions of agents.

Figure 1: The available versions of NetLogo

NetLogo has a Models Library with a large collection of agent-based models that can be used and/or modified. These address many areas in the natural and social sciences, including biology and medicine, physics and chemistry, mathematics and computer science, economics and social psychology. In addition, NetLogo can be used as classroom participatory-simulation tool by calling the special software module HubNet [23].

Netlogo uses three types of agents: turtles, patches and observer. When NetLogo is run first time, there are no turtles. The observer can create new turtles. In addition, the patches can do the same thing. Turtles and patches have coordinates determined by the variables *xcor* and *ycor* for turtles and, respectively, *pxcor* and *pycor* for patches. The patch with the coordinate *(0,0)* is called origin. *pxcor* is growing *(pxcor>0)* if we are moving to the right and is dropping *(pxcor<0)* if we are moving to the left in comparison with the origin. In the same time, *pycor* is growing *(pycor>0)* if we are moving up and is dropping *(pycor<0)* if we are moving down in comparison with the origin. The total number of patches is determined by the parameters *min-pxcor*, *max-pxcor*, *min-pycor* and *max-pycor*.

In NetLogo, the procedures are of two types: commands and reporters. A command is an action that an agent must execute. A reporter calculates a result and reports it. NetLogo uses four types of variables: global variables, turtles variables, patches variables and system variables. The first type of variables may be accessed by any type of agent. The next two types can be accessed only by the agent inside whom the variables were created. The last type of variables is predefined by NetLogo. Examples of system variable are the next: *color* (sets the color of turtle), *pcolor* (sets the color of patch), *xcor*, *ycor*, *heading* (sets the orientation in space of turtles), *pxcor*, *pycor,* etc.

In NetLogo, you have the choice of viewing models found in the Models Library, adding other models to existing ones, or creating your own models. The NetLogo interface was designed to meet all these needs. The interface is divided into two main parts: NetLogo menus and the main NetLogo window. The main window is divided into the next tabs: "Interface", "Procedures" and "Information". Only one tab at a time can be visible, but you can switch between them by clicking on the tabs at the top of the window. Right below the row of tabs is a toolbar containing a row of buttons. The available buttons vary from tab to tab. The "Interface" tab is where you watch the running of model. This tab also has tools that you can use to inspect and alter what is going on inside the model. When you first open NetLogo, the "Interface" tab is empty except for the View, where the turtles and patches appear, and the Command Center, which allows you to enter NetLogo commands.

The "Procedures" tab is the workspace where the code for the model is stored. The commands that you only want to use immediately go in the Command Center; the commands that you want to save and use later, over and over again, are found in the "Procedures" tab.

The "Information" tab provides an introduction to the model and an explanation of how to use it, things to explore, possible extensions, and NetLogo features.

NetLogo has the next defining characteristics:

(i)   Simplicity: NetLogo models are created without major technical difficulties and, under these conditions, the scientist can concentrate only on modeling problems. NetLogo offer a software platform that can be used even by no experienced programmers;

(ii) Transparency: NetLogo models contain only the elements that are explicitly included by modeler. Every element can be documented is accessible using NetLogo interface;

(iii) Gradual modeling: NetLogo permit a gradual development of models and by using this method you can avoid the traps of complexity;

(iv) Cross-platform: runs on Mac, Windows, Linux, etc;

(v)   Extensive options of running: any model can be run in many ways;

(vi) Environment: you can view your model in either 2D and 3D;

(vii) BehaviorSpace tool used to collect data from multiple runs of a model;

(viii) System Dynamics Modeler;

(ix) Speed slider lets you fast forward your model or see it in slow motion;

(x)   Powerful and flexible plotting system;

(xi) HubNet: participatory simulations using networked devices;

(xii) Models can be saved as applets to be embedded in web pages.

A GENERAL DESCRIPTION OF AAS MODEL

The model implemented in NetLogo is called AAS. AAS model uses the next types of agents:

- the observer that uses the parameters, variables and procedures presented in Table **1**;

- the patches that uses the parameters, variables and procedures described in Table **2**;

- the turtles that uses the parameters, variables and procedures from Table **3**.

Table 1: Parameters, variables and procedures used by observer

Label	Label used by NetLogo	Type	Description
t	ticks	global variable	the number of years
s	rs	global parameter	the seed of pseudo random number generator, $s \in \{-2,-1,0,1,2\}$
z	Renewable	global parameter	has two possible values 0 for nonrenewable resources and 1 for renewable resources
f	NoFemale	global parameter	the initial number of females, f=5
m	NoMale	global parameter	the initial number of males, m=5
n_t	NoTurtles	global variable	the number of turtles
f_t	Women	global variable	the number of females
m_t	Men	global variable	the number of males
v	MaxVision	global parameter	the maximum possible vision of turtles, v=15
E	LifeExpectancyMax	global parameter	maximum life expectancy, E=80

e	LifeExpectancyMin	global parameter	minimum life expectancy, e=30
A	AgeSexualActive	global parameter	the age when the sexual life starts, A=20
r	Interval	global parameter	the value of resources growth interval, $r \in \{1,2,3,4,5,6,7,8,9,10\}$
w_t	MeanWealthWater	global variable	mean wealth in water
f_t	MeanWealthFood	global variable	mean wealth in food
e_t	MeanWealthEnergy	global variable	mean wealth in energy
W_t	MeanGlobalWealth	global variable	mean global wealth
v^l_t	AvgVisionLow	global variable	the average vision for low class
v^m_t	AvgVisionMedium	global variable	the average vision for medium class
v^h_t	AvgVisionHigh	global variable	the average vision for high class
n^l_t	Low	global variable	the number of turtles from low class
n^m_t	Medium	global variable	the number of turtles from medium class
n^h_t	High	global variable	the number of turtles from high class
w^l_t	WealthLow	global variable	the average global wealth of low class
w^m_t	WealthMedium	global variable	global wealth of medium class
w^h_t	WealthHigh	global variable	global wealth of high class
InitPVA	globals[ ] patches-own[ ] turtles-own[ ]	Declarations	Initialization of parameters, variables and algorithms
Setup	Setup	global procedure	Setup of computer simulation
Go	Go	global procedure	Start of computer simulation

Table 2: Parameters, variables and procedures used by patches

Label	Label used by NetLogo	Type	Description
x	pxcor	patch variable	the horizontal coordinate of patch P_{xy}, $x \in [-10,10]$
y	pycor	patch variable	the vertical coordinate of patch P_{xy}, $y \in [-10,10]$
p_{xy}	TypePatch	patch parameter	the type of patch: "food" for food patch, "water" for water patch, and "energy" for energy patch
w^{xy}_t	ResWater	patch variable	the value of water resources
f^{xy}_t	ResFood	patch variable	the value of food resources
e^{xy}_t	ResEnergy	patch variable	the value of energy resources
PatchesCreation	PatchesCreation	patch procedure	Creates three types of patches: food, energy and water
GrowResource	GrowResource	patch procedure	Grows the resources at the beginning of every year

Table 3: Parameters, variables and procedures used by turtles

Label	Label used by NetLogo	Type	Description
i	who	turtle parameter	the identification number of the turtle, $i \in \{0,1,2,...,n_t-1\}$
x^i_t	xcor	turtle variable	the current x coordinate of the turtle
y^i_t	ycor	turtle variable	the current y coordinate of the turtle
h^i_t	heading	turtle variable	the direction the turtle is facing; This is a number greater than or equal to 0 and less than 360
f_i	IdMother	turtle parameter	the identification number of mother, $f_i \in \{0,1,2,...,n_t-1\}$
m_i	IdFather	turtle parameter	the identification number of father, $m_i \in \{0,1,2,...,n_t-1\}$
t_i	Age	turtle parameter	the age of the turtle

Table 3: cont....

E_i	LifeExpectancy	turtle parameter	maximum age that a turtle can reach, $E_i \in [e,E] \cap \mathbb{N}$
v_i	Vision	turtle parameter	the vision of the turtle (how many patches ahead a turtle can see for harvesting), $v_i \in \{1,2,...,v\}$
s_i	shape="woman" for s_i=0 and shape="man" for s_i=1	turtle parameter	a boolean parameter that have two possible values: 0 if the turtle is female and 1 if the turtle is male
g^i_t	WomanEngaged? when s_i=0 or ManEngaged? when s_i=1	turtle variable	a boolean variable that have two possible values: 0 if the turtle is not engaged in a relation and 1 if the turtle is engaged
p^i_t	IdHusband when s_i=0 or IdWife when s_i=1	turtle variable	the identification number of the sexual partner, $p_i \in \{0,1,2,...,n_t\text{-}1\}$
w^i_t	WealthWater	turtle variable	the quantity of water owned
f^i_t	WealthFood	turtle variable	the quantity of food owned
e^i_t	WealthEnergy	turtle variable	the quantity of energy owned
W^i_t	GlobalWealth	turtle variable	the global wealth
n^i_t	Pregnant?	turtle variable	a variable that have the next possible values: 0 if the turtle is not pregnant in a relation and 1 if the turtle is pregnant with female child and 2 if it is pregnant with male child
d^i_t	PregnancyDuration	turtle variable	pregnancy duration
c^i_t	SocialClass	turtle variable	the social class: 1 for low, 2 for medium and 3 for high
TurtlesCreation	TurtlesCreation	turtle procedure	Creates the initial number of turtles
FindResources	FindResources	turtle procedure	Used by turtles to find the available resources
FindWomen	FindWomen	turtle procedure	Used by male turtles to find an available female sexual partner
DoSex	DoSex	turtle procedure	Used to simulate the sexual relation within a couple
EatDrinkWarmAgeDie	EatDrinkWarmAgeDie	turtle procedure	Used to eat, drink, warm, age, leave the wealth to the inheritors and die
Pregnancy	Pregnancy	turtle procedure	Used to simulate the pregnancy period and the born of new turtles
UpdateSocialClass	UpdateSocialClass	turtle procedure	Used to update the social classes
InheritTurtle	InheritTurtle	turtle procedure	Used to find the available inheritors of turtle T_i
CountInheritors	CountInheritors	turtle procedure	Used to count the inheritors of turtle T_i
InheritOfTurtle	InheritOfTurtle	turtle procedure	Used to inherit the wealth of turtle T_i to its inheritors. Every inheritor will obtain w units of water, f units of food, and e units of energy

The AAS model implemented in NetLogo contains three tabs. First tab is the Interface tab is where you watch the model run – see (Fig. **2**), the second is Information tab provides an introduction to the model and an explanation of how to use it, things to explore, possible extensions, and NetLogo features – see (Fig. **3**), and the last is Procedures tab that is the workspace where the code for the model is stored – see (Fig. **4**).

A program written in NetLogo consists of optional declarations (globals, breed, turtles-own, patches-own, <BREED>-own) in any order, followed by zero or more procedure definitions. In NetLogo, there are two types of procedures: commands and reporters. A command is an action for an agent to carry out. A reporter computes a result and reports it. Multiple breeds may be declared with separate breed declarations; the other declarations may appear once only.

Every procedure definition begins with to or to-report, the procedure name, and an optional bracketed list of input names. Every procedure definition ends with end. In between are zero or more commands. Commands take zero or more inputs; the inputs are reporters, which may also take zero or more inputs. No punctuation separates or terminates commands; no punctuation separates inputs. Identifiers must be separated by whitespace or by parentheses or square brackets. (So for example, a+b is a single identifier, but a (b[c]d) e contains five identifiers.)

All commands are prefix. All user-defined reporters are prefix. Most primitive reporters are prefix, but some (arithmetic operators, Boolean operators, and some agent-set operators like with and in-points) are infix.

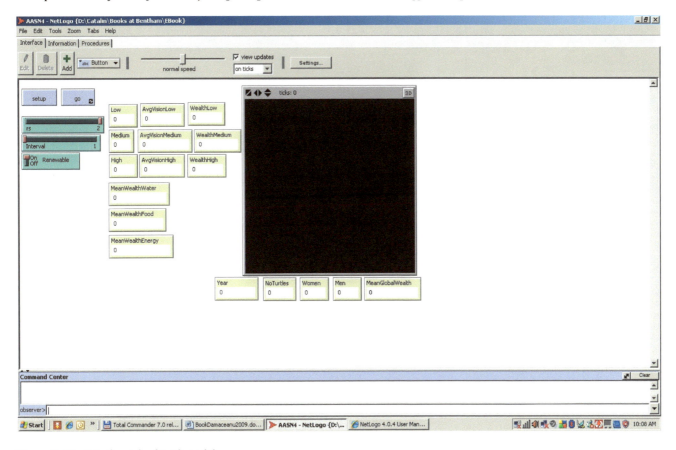

Figure 2: The Interface tab of AAS model

Figure 3: The Information tab of AAS model

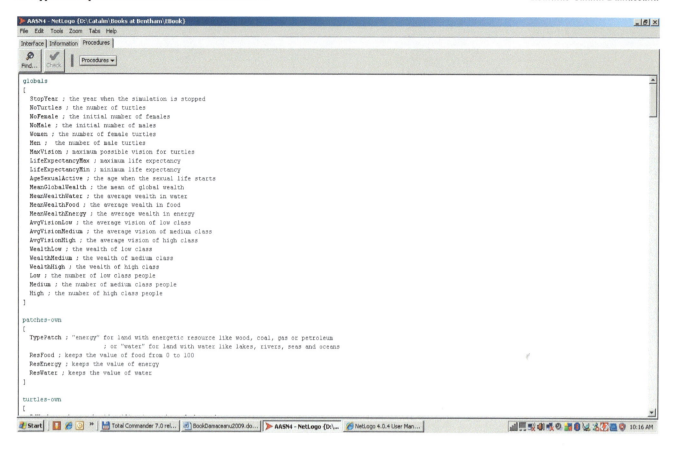

Figure 4: The Procedures tab of AAS model

All commands and reporters, both primitive and user-defined, take a fixed number of inputs by default. (That's why the language can be parsed though there is no punctuation to separate or terminate commands and/or inputs.) Some primitives are variadic, that is, may optionally take a different number of inputs than the default; parentheses are used to indicate this, e.g. (`list 1 2 3`) (since the list primitive only takes two inputs by default). Parentheses are also used to override the default operator precedence, e.g. `(1 + 2) * 3`, as in other programming languages.

Sometimes an input to a primitive is a command block (zero or more commands inside square brackets) or a reporter block (a single reporter expression inside square brackets). User-defined procedures may not take a command or reporter block as input.

Operator precedences are as follows, high to low:

(i)   with, at-points, in-radius, in-cone

(ii)   (all other primitives and user-defined procedures)

(iii)   ^

(iv)   *, /, mod

(v)   +, -

(vi)   <, >, <=, >=

(vii)   =, !=

(viii) and, or, xor

THE OBSERVER-OWN PROCEDURES

The observer-own procedures are the code lines written in NetLogo there are located in the next sections:

(i)   `globals[... ]`

(ii) `patches-own[... ]`

(iii) `turtles-own[ ...]`

(iv) `to Setup ... end`

(v)   `to Go .... end`

The keyword `globals[...]` can only be used at the beginning of a program, before any function definitions. It defines new global variables or parameters. Global variables are accessible by all agents and can be used anywhere in a model. Most often, `globals[...]` is used to define variables or constants that need to be used in many parts of the program. In our case, we defined the next new global variables and parameters: `StopYear` (the year when the simulation is stopped), `NoTurtles` (the number of turtles), `NoFemale` (the initial number of females), `NoMale` (the initial number of males), `Women` (the number of female turtles), `Men` (the number of male turtles), `MaxVision` (maximum possible vision for turtles), `LifeExpectancyMax` (maximum life expectancy), `LifeExpectancyMin` (minimum life expectancy), `AgeSexualActive` (the age when the sexual life starts), `MeanGlobalWealth` (the mean of global wealth), `MeanWealthWater` (the average wealth in water), `MeanWealthFood` (the average wealth in food), `MeanWealthEnergy` (the average wealth in energy), `AvgVisionLow` (the average vision of low class), `AvgVisionMedium` (the average vision of medium class), `AvgVisionHigh` (the average vision of high class), `WealthLow` (the wealth of low class), `WealthMedium` (the wealth of medium class), `WealthHigh` (the wealth of high class), `Low` (the number of low class people), `Medium` (the number of medium class people), and `High` (the number of high class people) – see the next code lines:

```
globals

    [

      StopYear ; the year when the simulation is stopped

      NoTurtles ; the number of turtles

      NoFemale ; the initial number of females

      NoMale ; the initial number of males

      Women ; the number of female turtles

      Men ;  the number of male turtles

      MaxVision ; maximum possible vision for turtles

      LifeExpectancyMax ; maximum life expectancy

      LifeExpectancyMin ; minimum life expectancy

      AgeSexualActive ; the age when the sexual life starts

      MeanGlobalWealth ; the mean of global wealth

      MeanWealthWater ; the average wealth in water

      MeanWealthFood ; the average wealth in food

      MeanWealthEnergy ; the average wealth in energy

      AvgVisionLow ; the average vision of low class

      AvgVisionMedium ; the average vision of medium class

      AvgVisionHigh ; the average vision of high class

      WealthLow ; the wealth of low class

      WealthMedium ; the wealth of medium class

      WealthHigh ; the wealth of high class

      Low ; the number of low class people
```

```
Medium ; the number of medium class people

High ; the number of high class people

]
```

The keyword `patches-own` can only be used at the beginning of a program, before any function definitions. It defines the variables and parameters that all patches can use. All patches will then have the given variables and be able to use them. All patch variables can also be directly accessed by any turtle standing on the patch. In our model, we defined the next patches-own variables and parameters: `TypePatch` (the type of patch), `ResFood` (the level of food resources), `ResEnergy` (keeps the value of energy resources), and `ResWater` (keeps the value of water resources) – see the next code lines:

```
patches-own

    [

        TypePatch ; the type of patch

        ResFood ; keeps the value of food resources

        ResEnergy ; keeps the value of energy resources

        ResWater ; keeps the value of water resources

    ]
```

The `turtles-own` keyword can only be used at the beginning of a program, before any function definitions. It defines the variables and parameters belonging to each turtle. Our model uses the next: `IdMother` (keeps the identification number of the mother), `IdFather` (keeps the identification number of the father), `Age` (age in years for every turtle), `LifeExpectancy` (maximum age that a turtle can reach), `Vision` (how many patches ahead a turtle can see), `WomanEngaged?` (used to prevent two males from engaging the same female), `IdHusband` (the identification number of the husband), `ManEngaged?` (used to prevent two females from engaging the same male), `IdWife` (the identification number of the wife), `WealthFood` (the quantity of food owned), `WealthEnergy` (the quantity of energy owned), `WealthWater` (the quantity of water owned), `GlobalWealth` (the global wealth), `Pregnant?` (has two possible values false for non pregnant woman and true otherwise), `PregnancyDuration` (the value of pregnancy duration), and `SocialClass` (the value of social class: low, middle and high) – see the next code lines.

```
turtles-own

    [

        IdMother ; keeps the identification number of the mother

        IdFather ; keeps the identification number of the father

        Age ; age in years for every turtle

        LifeExpectancy ; maximum age that a turtle can reach

        Vision ; how many patches ahead a turtle can see

        WomanEngaged? ; used to prevent two males from engaging the same female

        IdHusband ; the identification number of the husband

        ManEngaged? ; used to prevent two females from engaging the same male

        IdWife ; the identification number of the wife

        WealthFood ; the quantity of food owned

        WealthEnergy ; the quantity of energy owned

        WealthWater ; the quantity of water owned

        GlobalWealth ; the global wealth

        Pregnant? ; has two possible values false for non pregnant woman and true
            otherwise

        PregnancyDuration ; the value of pregnancy duration
```

```
       SocialClass          ; the value of social class: low, middle and high

   ]
```

The procedure `Setup` makes the necessary steps in order to initiate the computer simulation – see the code lines bellow. The keyword `to` is used to begin a command procedure. The first command is `ca` that resets all global variables to zero, and calls `reset-ticks` (resets the tick counter to zero), `clear-turtles` (kills all turtles and resets the who numbering, so the next turtle created will be turtle 0), `clear-patches` (clears the patches by resetting all patch variables to their default initial values, including setting their color to black), `clear-drawing` (clears all lines and stamps drawn by turtles), `clear-all-plots` (clears every plot in the model), and `clear-output` (Clears all text from the model's output area).

The next six lines of procedure Setup set the variables `StopYear`, `NoFemale`, `NoMale`, `MaxVision`, `LifeExpectancyMax`, `LifeExpectancyMin`, and `AgeSexualActive` to the given values.

The next line uses the command `random-seed` that sets the seed of the pseudo-random number generator. The seed may be any integer in the range supported by NetLogo (-9007199254740992 to 9007199254740992). The random numbers used by NetLogo are what is called "pseudo-random". That means they appear random, but are in fact generated by a deterministic process. "Deterministic" means that you get the same results every time, if you start with the same random "seed".

The next three lines call the procedures `PatchesCreation` (Creates three types of patches: food, energy and water), `TurtlesCreation` (Creates the initial number of turtles), and `UpdateSocialClass` (Used to update the social classes).

The next code line computes the number of turtles `NoTurtles` using the reporter `count turtles` that reports the total number of turtles. The next two lines use the same reporter to count the number of female turtles and male turtles.

The next four lines compute the average value of water wealth, food wealth, energy wealth, and global wealth using the reporter `mean` that reports the statistical mean of the numeric items in the given list.

The final line of procedure `Setup` is the keyword `end` used to conclude a procedure.

```
    to Setup
      ca
      set StopYear 1000
      set NoFemale 5
      set NoMale 5
      set MaxVision 15
      set LifeExpectancyMax 80
      set LifeExpectancyMin 30
      set AgeSexualActive 20
      random-seed rs ;; sets the random seed to a certain value in order that
        computational experiments to be reproducible
      PatchesCreation
      TurtlesCreation
      UpdateSocialClass
      set NoTurtles count turtles
      set Women count turtles with [shape = "woman"]
      set Men count turtles with [shape = "man"]
```

```
    set MeanWealthWater mean [WealthWater] of turtles
    set MeanWealthFood mean [WealthFood] of turtles
    set MeanWealthEnergy mean [WealthEnergy] of turtles
    set MeanGlobalWealth mean [GlobalWealth] of turtles
  end
```

The procedure Go starts the computer simulation. The first command is tick that advances the tick counter by one.

The next code line uses twice the reporter if that reports a Boolean (true or false) value. If condition reports true then it runs the commands between brackets. In our case if Interval = 0 and Renewable = true then it runs the procedure GrowResource.

The next code line is checking if the number of turtles is equal with zero and if this is true the simulation is stopped using the command stop that exits immediately from the enclosing procedure, ask, or ask-like construct (crt, hatch, sprout, without-interruption). Only the current procedure stops, not all execution for the agent. In our case stop is used to stop a forever button (Go). If the forever button directly calls a procedure, then when that procedure stops, the button stops. (In a turtle or patch forever button, the button won't stop until every turtle or patch stops - a single turtle or patch doesn't have the power to stop the whole button.)

The next line uses the command ask that runs the given commands for the specified agent or agentset. In our case all turtles run the next procedures: FindResources and EatDrinkWarmAgeDie.

The next line asks to all male turtles to run the procedure FindWomen if they are not engaged in other sexual relation and if they have a age higher or equal with AgeSexualActive.

The next line asks to all male turtles that are engaged in a sexual relation to run the procedure DoSex.

The next line runs the procedure UpdateSocialClass.

The next line computes the number of turtles, the number of female turtles and male turtles, the average value of water wealth, food wealth, energy wealth, and global wealth if the number of turtles is different of zero, otherwise the simulation is stopped.

The last line stops the simulation if ticks reports StopYear. ticks reports the current value of the tick counter. The result is always a number and never negative. Most models use tick command to advance the tick counter, in which case ticks will always report an integer. If the tick-advance command is used, then ticks may report a floating point number.

```
  to Go
    tick
    if ticks mod (Interval) = 0
      [if Renewable [GrowResource]]
    if count turtles = 0 [ stop]
    ask turtles
      [FindResources
       EatDrinkWarmAgeDie]
    ask turtles with [shape = "man"]
      [if (ManEngaged? = false and Age >= AgeSexualActive) [ FindWomen ]]
    ask turtles with [shape = "man" and ManEngaged? = true] [DoSex]
    UpdateSocialClass
```

```
  if-else count turtles != 0
   [set NoTurtles count turtles
    set MeanWealthWater mean [WealthWater] of turtles
    set MeanWealthFood mean [WealthFood] of turtles
    set MeanWealthEnergy mean [WealthEnergy] of turtles
    set MeanGlobalWealth mean [GlobalWealth] of turtles
    set Women count turtles with [shape = "woman"]
    set Men count turtles with [shape = "man"]]
   [stop]
  if ticks = StopYear [stop]
 end
```

THE PATCHES-OWN PROCEDURES

There are three patches-own procedures: PatchesCreation, GrowResource, and RecolorPatch. The first one is used when all the patches are created – see the next code lines. This procedure uses a local variable Prob that is set to the value 0. The next code line ask all patches to set this local variable to a random value using the reporter random 3 that reports a random integer greater than or equal to 0 but strictly less than 3. If Prob = 0 then the respective patch is a "food" patch and holds food resources (ResFood>0). If Prob = 1 then the respective patch is a "energy" patch (ResEnergy>0). If Prob = 2 then the respective patch is a "water" patch (ResWater>0).

After all patches are created then this procedure is checking if the number of "food" patches or "energy" patches or "water" patches is equal with zero or no. If this is true then the procedure PatchesCreation is rerun.

```
  to PatchesCreation
    let Prob 0
    ask patches
     [set Prob random 3
      if (Prob = 0)
       [set TypePatch "food"
        set ResFood (1 + random 10)
        set ResEnergy 0
        set ResWater 0]
      if (Prob = 1)
       [set TypePatch "energy"
        set ResFood 0
        set ResEnergy (1 + random 10)
        set ResWater 0]
      if (Prob = 2)
       [set TypePatch "water"
        set ResFood 0
        set ResEnergy 0
        set ResWater (1 + random 10)]]
    if (count patches with [TypePatch = "water"] = 0)
```

```
          or (count patches with [TypePatch = "food"] = 0)
          or (count patches with [TypePatch = "energy"] = 0)
            [PatchesCreation]
      ask patches
        [RecolorPatch]
    end
```

The other procedure `GrowResource` is used when the resources are renewed in function of parameter `Interval` when the parameter `Renewable` has the value `true`.

```
    to GrowResource
      ask patches
        [if (TypePatch = "food")
          [set ResFood (ResFood + 1 + random 10)]
         if (TypePatch = "energy")
          [set ResEnergy (ResEnergy 1 + random 10)]
         if (TypePatch = "water")
          [set ResWater (ResWater + 1 + random 10)]]
    end
```

The third procedure `RecolorPatch` recolor the patch by using the reporter `scale-color color number range1 range2` that reports a shade of `color` proportional to `number`. If `range1` is less than `range2`, then the larger the number, the lighter the shade of `color`. But if `range2` is less than `range1`, the color scaling is inverted. If `number` is less than `range1`, then the darkest shade of `color` is chosen. If `number` is greater than `range2`, then the lightest shade of `color` is chosen.

```
    to RecolorPatch
      if (TypePatch = "food")
        [set pcolor scale-color green ResFood 0 10]
      if (TypePatch = "water")
        [set pcolor scale-color blue ResWater 0 10]
      if (TypePatch = "energy")
        [set pcolor scale-color yellow ResEnergy 0 10]
    end
```

THE TURTLES-OWN PROCEDURES

There are ten turtles-own procedures: `TurtlesCreation`, `FindResources`, `FindWomen`, `DoSex`, `EatDrinkWarmAgeDie`, `Pregnancy`, `UpdateSocialClass`, `InheritTurtle`, `CountInheritors`, and `InheritOfTurtle`. The first procedure `TurtlesCreation` uses the command `crt number [ commands ]` that creates *number* new turtles. If *commands* are supplied, the new turtles immediately run *commands*. Between these commands, there is used a built-in turtle variable shape that holds a string with the name of the turtle's current shape. You can set this variable to change the shape. New turtles have the shape "default" unless a different shape has been specified using set-default-shape. NetLogo has a turtle shape editor that allows you to create and save turtle designs. NetLogo uses fully scalable and rotatable vector shapes, which means you can create designs by combining basic geometric elements, which can appear on-screen in any size or orientation. Another command is `setxy x y` that sets its x-coordinate to x and its y-coordinate to y. Equivalent to `set xcor x set ycor y`, except it happens in one time step instead of two. If x or y is outside the world, NetLogo will throw a runtime error.

```
to TurtlesCreation
  crt NoFemale
    [set shape "woman"
     set color pink
     set IdMother false
     set IdFather false
     set Age 20
     set WomanEngaged? false
     set IdHusband false
     set WealthFood 10
     set WealthEnergy 10
     set WealthWater 10
     set GlobalWealth WealthFood + WealthEnergy + WealthWater
     set LifeExpectancy 1 + LifeExpectancyMin + random (LifeExpectancyMax -
     LifeExpectancyMin)
     set Vision 1 + random MaxVision
     set size 1
     set Pregnant? false
     set PregnancyDuration false
     setxy 0 0]
  crt NoMale
    [set IdMother false
     set IdFather false
     set shape "man"
     set Age 20
     set ManEngaged? false
     set IdWife false
     set WealthFood 10
     set WealthEnergy 10
     set WealthWater 10
     set GlobalWealth WealthFood + WealthEnergy + WealthWater
     set LifeExpectancy 1 + LifeExpectancyMin + random (LifeExpectancyMax -
     LifeExpectancyMin)
     set color red
     set size 1
     set Vision 1 + random MaxVision
     setxy 0 0]
  end
```

The second procedure FindResources is used by turtles to find the available resources in order to survive. This procedure uses a local variable Resource, initially set to zero value.

The next line sets a random direction where the turtle is facing. The following line use the command `repeat` *number* `[` *commands* `]` that runs *commands* for *number* times. The first command between brackets is `fd` *number* that moves forward by *number* steps, one step at a time. The next commands are used to harvest the resources available on the patch where the turtle is sitting and finally the procedure `RecolorPatch` is run.

```
to FindResources
   let Resource 0
   set heading random 360
   repeat Vision
   [fd 1
     set Resource ResFood / count turtles-here
     set WealthFood WealthFood + Resource
     set ResFood ResFood - Resource
     set Resource ResEnergy / count turtles-here
     set WealthEnergy WealthEnergy + Resource
     set ResEnergy ResEnergy - Resource
     set Resource ResWater / count turtles-here
     set WealthWater WealthWater + Resource
     set ResWater ResWater - Resource
     RecolorPatch]
end
```

The third procedure FindWomen is used by male turtles that are sexual active are not engaged in other sexual relation to find female turtles that are also sexual active and not engaged in other relation. This procedure uses the reporter one-of *agentset* that reports a random agent from an *agentset*. If the *agentset* is empty, reports nobody.

In addition, there is used [*reporter*] of *agent* that reports the value of the reporter for that agent.

```
to FindWomen
   let Engage one-of turtles with
     [shape = "woman" and WomanEngaged? = false and Age >= AgeSexualActive]
   if Engage != nobody
   [set [WomanEngaged?] of Engage true
     set ManEngaged? true
     set IdWife [who] of Engage
     set [IdHusband] of Engage who]
end
```

The fourth procedure is used to simulate to simulate the sexual relation between one male turtle and one female turtle. This procedure uses a local variable `Sex` that have a random value from the set {0,1,2}. If `Sex = 1` or `Sex = 2` then the female turtle remains pregnant.

```
to DoSex
   let Sex random 3
   if Sex = 1 or Sex = 2
```

```
        [let WhoMale who
          ask turtles with
            [shape = "woman"
             and IdHusband = WhoMale
             and Pregnant? = false]
            [set Pregnant? Sex
             set PregnancyDuration 0]]
   end
```

The fifth procedure is used by turtles to eat, drink, warm, age, leave the wealth to the inheritors and die. The first line of this procedure is checking if `WealthFood >= 1` and if this is true then `WealthFood` is decremented, otherwise procedure `InheritTurtle` is run and after it the respective turtle dies using the command `die`.

The same checking is performed for variables `WealthWater` and `WealthEnergy`. If these variables are higher or equal with one then they are decremented, otherwise the procedure `InheritTurtle` is run and the respective turtle dies.

The next line is incrementing the age of turtle.

If the turtle is female then if she is pregnant the procedure `Pregnancy` is run.

If the age is higher then the life expectancy the procedure `InheritTurtle` is run and the respective turtle dies.

```
   to EatDrinkWarmAgeDie
     if-else WealthFood >= 1
       [set WealthFood WealthFood - 1]
       [InheritTurtle
        die]
     if-else WealthWater >= 1
       [set WealthWater WealthWater - 1]
       [InheritTurtle
        die]
     if-else WealthEnergy >= 1
       [set WealthEnergy WealthEnergy - 1]
       [InheritTurtle
        die]
     set Age Age + 1
     if shape = "woman" [if Pregnant? != false [Pregnancy]]
     if Age >= LifeExpectancy
       [InheritTurtle
        die]
   end
```

The sixth procedure is `Pregnancy` used for to simulate the pregnancy period and the born of new turtles.

The first line is used for incrementing the variable `PregnancyDuration`.

If PregnancyDuration >= 1 then the respective female turtle born a new turtle using the command hatch *number* [*commands*] that creates *number* new turtles. Each new turtle is identical to, and at the same location as, its parent. The new turtles then run *commands*. You can use the *commands* to give to new turtles different colors, headings, locations, or whatever. The new turtles are created all at once, then run one at a time, in random order.

```
to Pregnancy
 set PregnancyDuration PregnancyDuration + 1
 if PregnancyDuration >= 1
    [let Sex Pregnant?
     set Pregnant? false
     set PregnancyDuration false
     let Mother who
     let WealthFoodMother WealthFood
     let WealthEnergyMother WealthEnergy
     let WealthWaterMother WealthWater
     set WealthFood WealthFood * 9 / 10
     set WealthEnergy WealthEnergy * 9 / 10
     set WealthWater WealthWater * 9 / 10
     let VisionMother Vision
     let Father false
     let WealthFoodFather 0
     let WealthEnergyFather 0
     let WealthWaterFather 0
     let VisionFather 0
     ask turtles with [shape = "man" and IdWife = Mother]
       [set Father who
        set WealthFoodFather WealthFood
        set WealthEnergyFather WealthEnergy
        set WealthWaterFather WealthWater
        set WealthFood WealthFood * 9 / 10
        set WealthEnergy WealthEnergy * 9 / 10
        set WealthWater WealthWater * 9 / 10
        set VisionFather Vision]
      if Sex = 1
      [hatch 1
         [set shape "woman"
          set size 1
          set color pink
          set IdMother Mother
          set IdFather Father
          set Age 0
```

```
        set WomanEngaged? false

        set IdHusband false

        set WealthFood (WealthFoodMother + WealthFoodFather) / 10

        set WealthEnergy (WealthEnergyMother + WealthEnergyFather) / 10

        set WealthWater (WealthWaterMother + WealthWaterFather) / 10

        set GlobalWealth WealthFood + WealthEnergy + WealthWater

        set LifeExpectancy 1 + LifeExpectancyMin + random (LifeExpectancyMax
 - LifeExpectancyMin)

        set Vision 1 + random MaxVision

        set Pregnant? false

        set PregnancyDuration false]]
      if sex = 2
       [hatch 1
        [set shape "man"

         set size 1

         set IdMother Mother

         set IdFather Father

         set color red

         set Age 0

         set ManEngaged? false

         set IdWife false

         set WealthFood (WealthFoodMother + WealthFoodFather) / 10

         set WealthEnergy (WealthEnergyMother + WealthEnergyFather) / 10

         set WealthWater (WealthWaterMother + WealthWaterFather) / 10

         set GlobalWealth WealthFood + WealthEnergy + WealthWater

         set LifeExpectancy 1 + LifeExpectancyMin + random (LifeExpectancyMax
 - LifeExpectancyMin)

         set Vision 1 + random MaxVision]]]
   end
```

The seventh procedure `UpdateSocialClass` is used to update the social classes. There are counted the turtles that are included in low, medium, and high social class. In addition, the average vision and wealth are computed for each social class.

```
to UpdateSocialClass
   if count turtles = 0 [stop]
   ask turtles
    [set GlobalWealth WealthFood + WealthEnergy + WealthWater]
   let MaxWealth max [GlobalWealth] of turtles
   ask turtles
    [ifelse (GlobalWealth <= MaxWealth / 3)
     [set SocialClass "low" ]
```

```
    [ifelse (GlobalWealth <= (MaxWealth * 2 / 3))

     [set SocialClass "medium" ]

     [set SocialClass "high"]]]

  set Low count turtles with [SocialClass = "low"]

  set Medium count turtles with [SocialClass = "medium"]

  set High count turtles with [SocialClass = "high"]

  if Low != 0

   [set AvgVisionLow mean [vision] of turtles with [SocialClass = "low"]

    set WealthLow mean [GlobalWealth] of turtles with [SocialClass = "low"]]

  if Medium != 0

   [set AvgVisionMedium mean [vision] of turtles with [SocialClass =
   "medium"]

    set WealthMedium mean [GlobalWealth] of turtles with [SocialClass =
    "medium"]]

  if High != 0

   [set AvgVisionHigh mean [vision] of turtles with [SocialClass = "high"]

    set WealthHigh mean [GlobalWealth] of turtles with [SocialClass =
    "high"]]

  end
```

The eighth procedure `InheritTurtle` is used to find the available inheritors of turtle. This procedure uses the next local variables: `InheritWater`, `InheritFood`, `InheritEnergy`, and `NoInheriters`. The last local variable is computed using the reporter procedure `CountInheritors who` that counts the number of inheritors for the respective turtle.

```
  to InheritTurtle

    let InheritWater 0

    let InheritFood 0

    let InheritEnergy 0

    let NoInheriters CountInheritors who

    if NoInheriters > 0

     [set InheritWater WealthWater / NoInheriters

      set InheritFood WealthFood / NoInheriters

      set InheritEnergy WealthFood / NoInheriters]

    let InheritAction false

    if NoInheriters > 0

     [set InheritAction InheritOfTurtle who InheritWater InheritFood
     InheritEnergy]

    if-else InheritAction = true

     []

     [let Water WealthWater

      let Food WealthFood

      let Energy WealthEnergy
```

```
      ask one-of patches with [TypePatch = "water"]
        [set ResWater ResWater + Water
         RecolorPatch]
      ask one-of patches with [TypePatch = "food"]
        [set ResFood ResFood + Food
         RecolorPatch]
      ask one-of patches with [TypePatch = "energy"]
        [set ResEnergy ResEnergy + Energy
         RecolorPatch]]
  end
```

The ninth procedure is `CountInheritors [a]`. This is a reporter procedure that has one input parameter `[a]`, uses one local variable `total` to compute the number inheritors, and report this number using the command report *value* that immediately exits from the current `to-report` procedure and reports *value* as the result of that procedure. `report` and `to-report` are always used in conjunction with each other.

```
  to-report CountInheritors [a]
    let total 0
    ask turtles with
      [IdFather = a or IdMother = a]
      [if IdFather = a or IdMother = a
       [set Total Total + 1
         ]]
    report Total
  end
```

The tenth procedure is `InheritOfTurtle` that uses four input parameters `[a b c d]`. This procedure finds all turtles inheritors of turtle with `who = a` and every inheritors takes b units of water, c units of food and d units of energy.

```
  to-report InheritOfTurtle [a b c d]
    let Answer false
    ask turtles with [IdFather = a or IdMother = a]
      [set WealthWater WealthWater + b
       set WealthFood WealthFood + c
       set WealthEnergy WealthEnergy + d
       set Answer true]
    report Answer
  end
```

REFERENCES

[1]   Edmonds B. The Use of Models - making MABS actually work. In Moss S and Davidsson P (Eds.). Multi-Agent-Based Simulation, Lecture Notes in Artificial Intelligence 79: 15-32. Berlin: Springer-Verlag; 2001.

[2]   Gilbert N. Agent-Based Models. Quantitative Applications in the Social Sciences. London: SAGE Publications; 2007.

[3]   Axelrod RM. Advancing the Art of Simulation in the Social Sciences. In Conte R, Hegselmann R, Terna P. (Eds.). Simulating Social Phenomena. Lecture Notes in Economics and Mathematical Systems 456: 21-40. Berlin: Springer-Verlag; 1997.

[4]   Axtell RL, Epstein JM. Agent-based Modeling: Understanding Our Creations. The Bulletin of the Santa Fe Institute. 1994 Winter: 28-32.

[5]   Drogoul A, Vanbergue D, Meurisse T. Multi-Agent Based Simulation: Where are the Agents? In Sichman JS, Bousquet F, Davidsson P (Eds.). Multi-Agent Simulation II. Third International Workshop, MABS 2002: 1-15. Bologna, Italy: Springer-Verlag; 2003.

[6]   Christley S, Xiang X, Madey G. Ontology for agent-based modeling and simulation. In Macal CM, Sallach D, North MJ (Eds.). Proceedings of the Agent 2004 Conference on Social Dynamics: Interaction, Reflexivity and Emergence: Chicago, IL: Argonne National Laboratory and The University of Chicago. http://www.agent2005.anl.gov/Agent2004.pdf; 2004.

[7]   Pignotti E, Edwards P, Preece A, Polhill JG, Gotts NM. Semantic support for computational land-use modelling. 5th International Symposium on Cluster Computing and the Grid (CCGRID 2005): 840-847. Piscataway, NJ: IEEE Press; 2005.

[8]   Polhill JG, Gotts NM. A new approach to modelling frameworks. Proceedings of the First World Congress on Social Simulation. 50-57. Kyoto; 2006.

[9]   Polhill JG, Pignotti E, Gotts NM, Edwards P, Preece A. A Semantic Grid Service for Experimentation with an Agent-Based Model of Land-Use Change. Journal of Artificial Societies and Social Simulation 2007: 10(2) http://jasss.soc.surrey.ac.uk/10/2/2.html.

[10]   Gruber TR. A translation approach to portable ontology specifications. Knowledge Acquisition 1993 5(2): 199-220.

[11]   Kleijnen JPC.Verification and validation of simulation models. European Journal of Operational Research. 1995; 82(1): 145-162.

[12]   Sargent RG, Verification and Validation of Simulation Models. In Chick S, Sánchez P J, Ferrin D, and Morrice D J (Eds.) Proceedings of the 2003 Winter Simulation Conference: 37-48. Piscataway, NJ: IEEE; 2003.

[13]   Moss S, Edmonds B, Wallis S. Validation and Verification of Computational Models with Multiple Cognitive Agents. Centre for Policy Modelling Report 1997: 97-25, http://cfpm.org/cpmrep25.html.

[14]   Taylor AJ. The Verification of Dynamic Simulation Models. Journal of the Operational Research Society 1983 34(3): 233-42.

[15]   Sansores C, Pavón J. Agent-based simulation replication: A model driven architecture approach. In Gelbukh AF, de Albornoz A, and Terashima-Marín H (Eds.). MICAI 2005: Advances in Artificial Intelligence, 4th Mexican International Conference on Artificial Intelligence, Monterrey, Mexico, November 14-18, 2005, Proceedings. Lecture Notes in Computer Science 3789: 244-53. Berlin Heidelberg: Springer; 2005.

[16]   Stanislaw H. Tests of computer simulation validity. What do they measure? Simulation and Gaming 1986 17: 173-91.

[17]   Richiardi M, Leombruni R, Saam NJ, Sonnessa M. A Common Protocol for Agent-Based Social Simulation. Journal of Artificial Societies and Social Simulation. 2006 9(1): 15 http://jasss.soc.surrey.ac.uk/9/1/15.html.

[18]   Polhill JG, Izquierdo LR and Gotts NM. The ghost in the model (and other effects of floating point arithmetic). Journal of Artificial Societies and Social Simulation. 2005 8(1): http://jasss.soc.surrey.ac.uk/8/1/5.html.

[19]   Polhill JG, Izquierdo LR. Lessons learned from converting the artificial stock market to interval arithmetic. Journal of Artificial Societies and Social Simulation. 2005 8(2): http://jasss.soc.surrey.ac.uk/8/2/2.html.

[20]   Polhill JG, Izquierdo LR, Gotts NM. What every agent-based modeller should know about floating point arithmetic. Environmental Modelling & Software. 2006 21(3): 283-309.

[21]   Izquierdo LR., Polhill JG. Is your model susceptible to floating point errors?, Journal of Artificial Societies and Social Simulation. 2006 9(4): http://jasss.soc.surrey.ac.uk/9/4/4.html.

[22]   Wilensky U. NetLogo. http://ccl.northwestern.edu/netlogo/, Center for Connected Learning and Computer-Based Modeling. Evanston, IL: Northwestern University; 1999.

[23]   Wilensky U, Stroup W. HubNet. http://ccl.northwestern.edu/netlogo/hubnet.html. Center for Connected Learning and CoWilensky U. NetLogo. http://ccl.northwestern.edu/netlogo/, Center for Connected Learning and Computer-Based Modeling,; Evanston, IL: Northwestern University; 1999.

CHAPTER 4

The Computational Experiments Done with the Artificial Society Using Netlogo

Abstract: A computational experiment uses a computer model to make inferences about some underlying system. This type of experiment can be seen as a branch of applied statistics, because the user must take into account three sources of uncertainty. First, the models often contain parameters whose values are not certain; second, the models themselves are imperfect representations of the underlying system; and third, data collected from the system that might be used to calibrate the models are imperfectly measured. Study of multiple experiments involves two aspects: experimental planning, and analysis and modeling of experimental results. In this chapter, we will do 6 computer experiments containing 55 runs with our multi-agent based artificial society.

In the scientific context, a computational experiment or a computer experiment typically implies two phases. The modeling phase and the experimentation phase [1]. In such experiment a computer model is used to make inferences about a system. The computer model takes the place of an experiment we cannot do. Under these circumstances, the phrase in silico experiment is used [2].

Computational experiments can be seen as a branch of applied statistics, because the user must take into account the next sources of uncertainty:

(i)   First, the models may contain parameters whose values are not certain;

(ii) Second, the models themselves are imperfect representations of the studied system;

(iii) Third, data collected from the system that might be used to calibrate the models are imperfectly measured.

However, most practitioners of computational experiments do not see themselves as statisticians [3].

Experimentation to study complex systems can be conducted at different levels of accuracy or sophistication. Complex mathematical models, implemented in large computer codes, are used as a tool to study such systems. Doing the corresponding physical experiments would be costly [4].

Study of multiple computational experiments involves two aspects:

(i)   Experimental planning;

(ii) Analysis and modeling of experimental results [5].

The main reason of a simulation project is to run your model(s) and to try to understand the results. To do so effectively, you need to plan ahead before doing the runs, since just trying different things to see what happens can be a very inefficient way of attempting to learn about your models or systems behaviors. Careful planning of your experiments will generally give you positive results in terms of how effectively you learn about the system(s) and how you can develop your model(s) further - see [6-12].

PLANNING OF COMPUTER EXPERIMENTS

In this chapter, we will do 6 computer experiments described in Table **1**.

Table 1: The description of computer experiments `E1-E6`

Name	Description
E1	This experiment has 10 runs; the vary parameters are the next: `StopYear = 1000, Renewable = true, rs = -2, interval = {1, 2, 3, 4, 5, 6, 7, 8, 9, 10}`. The measured variables are the next: `ticks, NoTurtles, Women, Men, MeanGlobalWealth, Low, Medium, High, AvgVisionLow, AvgVisionMedium, AvgVisionHigh, WealthLow, WealthMedium,` and `WealthHigh`
E2	This experiment has 10 runs; the vary parameters are the next: `StopYear = 1000, Renewable = true, rs = -1, interval = {1, 2, 3, 4, 5, 6, 7, 8, 9, 10}`. The measured variables are the next: `ticks, NoTurtles, Women, Men, MeanGlobalWealth, Low, Medium, High, AvgVisionLow, AvgVisionMedium, AvgVisionHigh, WealthLow, WealthMedium,` and `WealthHigh`

Table 1: cont....

E3	This experiment has 10 runs; the vary parameters are the next: `StopYear = 1000, Renewable = true, rs = 0, interval = {1, 2, 3, 4, 5, 6, 7, 8, 9, 10}`. The measured variables are the next: `ticks, NoTurtles, Women, Men, MeanGlobalWealth, Low, Medium, High, AvgVisionLow, AvgVisionMedium, AvgVisionHigh, WealthLow, WealthMedium`, and `WealthHigh`
E4	This experiment has 10 runs; the vary parameters are the next: `StopYear = 1000, Renewable = true, rs = 1, interval = {1, 2, 3, 4, 5, 6, 7, 8, 9, 10}`. The measured variables are the next: `ticks, NoTurtles, Women, Men, MeanGlobalWealth, Low, Medium, High, AvgVisionLow, AvgVisionMedium, AvgVisionHigh, WealthLow, WealthMedium`, and `WealthHigh`
E5	This experiment has 10 runs; the vary parameters are the next: `StopYear = 1000, Renewable = true, rs = 2, interval = {1, 2, 3, 4, 5, 6, 7, 8, 9, 10}`. The measured variables are the next: `ticks, NoTurtles, Women, Men, MeanGlobalWealth, Low, Medium, High, AvgVisionLow, AvgVisionMedium, AvgVisionHigh, WealthLow, WealthMedium`, and `WealthHigh`
E6	This experiment has 5 runs; the vary parameters are the next: `StopYear = 1000, Renewable = false, rs = {-2, -1, 0, 1, 2}, interval = 1`. The measured variables are the next: `ticks, NoTurtles, Women, Men, MeanGlobalWealth, Low, Medium, High, AvgVisionLow, AvgVisionMedium, AvgVisionHigh, WealthLow, WealthMedium`, and `WealthHigh`

These 6 computer experiments are run using the BehaviorSpace tool located in Tools menu of NetLogo interface – see (Fig. **1**). If you select this option on the computer screen will appear the BahaviorSpace window. In this window, there is a list of computer experiments - see (Fig. **2**). You must select one of them and after this selection you can press Run button. If you pressed this button, then a new window will appear on the screen asking you to select in which type of format do you want to save the simulation results - see (Fig. **3**). You must select Table option and after it, you can press OK button and a new window is on the computer screen asking you to enter the name of the file that will store the simulation results (E1.csv) – see (Fig. **4**). After you entered the name of the file, then press Save button and the simulation will start – see (Fig. **5**).

The same procedure must be followed for the other five experiments (`E2-E6`). The results of these computer experiments are stored in Comma Separated Values (CSV) files. This is a plain-text data format that is readable by any text editor as well as by most popular spreadsheet and database programs – see (Figs. 6 and 7).

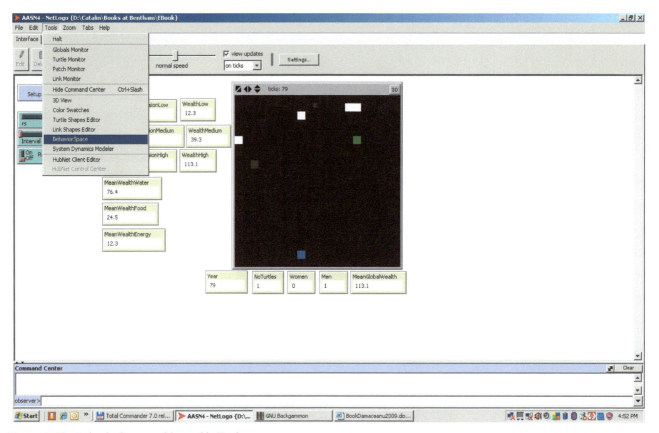

Figure 1: The BehaviorSpace tool located in Tools menu

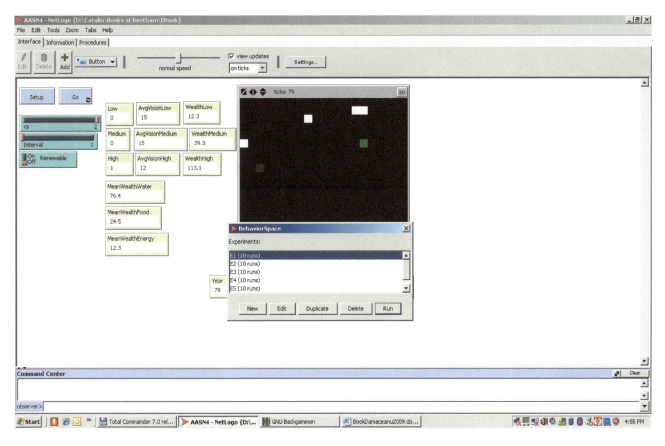

Figure 2: The BehaviorSpace window

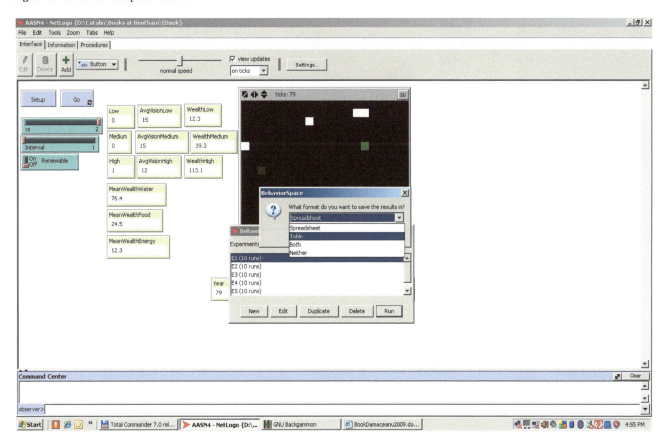

Figure 3: The window where you can select in which type of format do you want to save the simulation results.

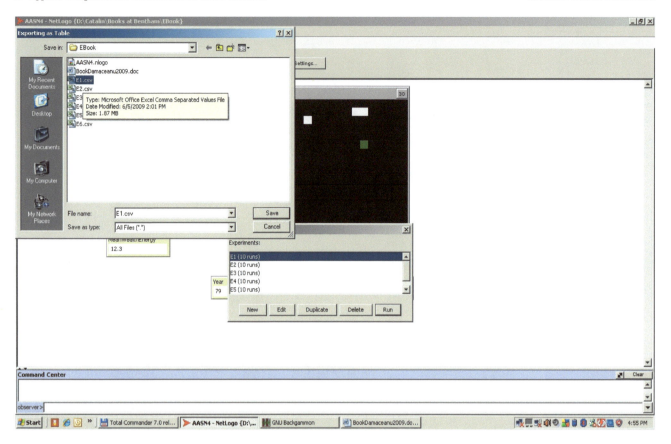

Figure 4: The window where you can introduce the name of the file that will store the simulation results

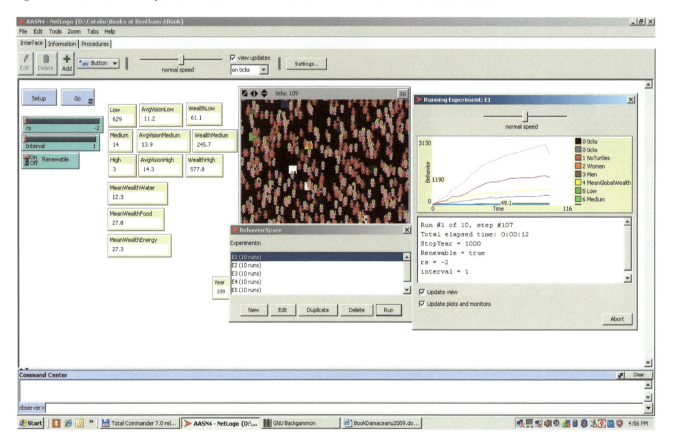

Figure 5: The window where you can see your computer experiment running

Figure 6: The plain text data format of `E1.csv` file

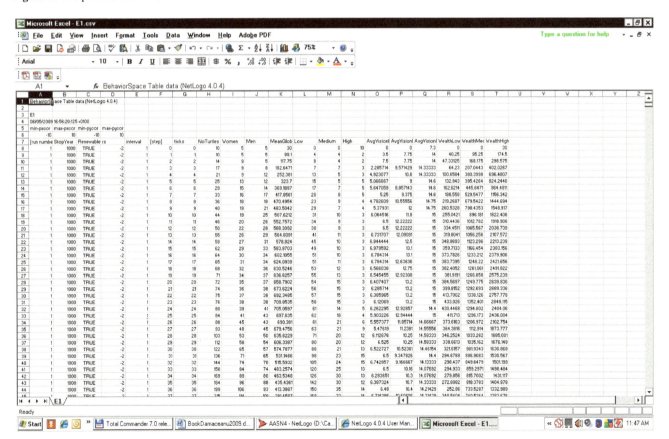

Figure 7: The results of computational experiment `E1` stored in `E1.csv` file are readable using Microsoft Excel

THE RESULTS OF COMPUTER EXPERIMENTS IN THE CASE WHEN RESOURCES ARE RENEWABLE

The results of these six computational experiments are presented in Appendix 1. The first five experiments are dealing with the case when resources are renewable. Based on data obtained after running these five experiments, we computed a new set of data that contain average values for the variables NoTurtles, Women, Men, MeanGlobalWealth, Low, Medium, High, AvgVisionLow, AvgVisionMedium, AvgVisionHigh, WealthLow, WealthMedium, and WealthHigh – see Appendix 2 for the evolution in time of these variables and Tables 2 – 14 for the average values in the case when resources are renewable.

Table 2: The average values of NoTurtles for the different values of Interval and rs

Interval	rs = -2	rs = -1	rs = 0	rs = 1	rs = 2	Mean
1	781.436	766.721	771.855	798.791	802.072	784.175
2	388.246	379.254	384.709	397.87	396.374	389.2906
3	258.224	253.451	255.581	264.846	263.991	259.2186
4	194.452	190.825	190.838	199.779	197.452	194.6692
5	155.779	151.838	152.986	158.385	157.347	155.267
6	128.833	126.72	127.342	131.532	131.398	129.165
7	110.443	108.623	109.096	112.531	113.456	110.8298
8	96.902	94.535	95.253	99.414	98.023	96.8254
9	86.277	84.211	84.753	87.522	86.273	85.8072
10	78.286	75.24	76.514	78.668	78.39	77.4196

Table 3: The average values of Women for the different values of Interval and rs

Interval	rs = -2	rs = -1	rs = 0	rs = 1	rs = 2	Mean
1	387.873	379.707	381.584	403.347	406.719	391.846
2	198.153	195.366	193.152	197.886	198.36	196.5834
3	128.752	128.24	127.285	130.875	130.6	129.1504
4	97.197	94.939	93.757	101.872	97.483	97.0496
5	77.979	76.146	78.201	79.305	80.129	78.352
6	63.246	63.053	63.651	65.328	67.381	64.5318
7	57.035	55.22	53.415	55.002	57.1	55.5544
8	48.506	49.047	48.342	49.483	49.878	49.0512
9	43.728	40.799	42.212	43.175	44.481	42.879
10	37.557	38.391	37.895	38.817	39.546	38.4412

Table 4: The average values of Men for the different values of Interval and rs

Interval	rs = -2	rs = -1	rs = 0	rs = 1	rs = 2	Mean
1	393.563	387.014	390.271	395.444	395.353	392.329
2	190.093	183.888	191.557	199.984	198.014	192.7072
3	129.472	125.211	128.296	133.971	133.391	130.0682
4	97.255	95.886	97.081	97.907	99.969	97.6196
5	77.8	75.692	74.785	79.08	77.218	76.915
6	65.587	63.667	63.691	66.204	64.017	64.6332
7	53.408	53.403	55.681	57.529	56.356	55.2754
8	48.396	45.488	46.911	49.931	48.145	47.7742
9	42.549	43.412	42.541	44.347	41.792	42.9282
10	40.729	36.849	38.619	39.851	38.844	38.9784

Table 5: The average values of `MeanGlobalWealth` for the different values of `Interval` and `rs`

Interval	rs = -2	rs = -1	rs = 0	rs = 1	rs = 2	Mean
1	152.428	112.7824	150.6915	138.2312	96.02994	130.0326
2	156.292	113.583	149.3117	132.3943	93.27044	128.9703
3	158.7869	115.164	154.8178	131.9473	94.02279	130.9478
4	151.3955	109.7153	154.059	132.0923	95.97186	128.6468
5	152.5799	117.1603	157.1186	137.0511	101.7599	133.134
6	164.8693	111.9008	154.474	142.5801	99.91231	134.7473
7	166.4021	110.1045	167.0717	163.2899	94.53955	140.2816
8	164.0281	129.1808	157.8085	146.729	105.5314	140.6555
9	156.3443	120.9557	158.3939	158.0738	99.20442	138.5944
10	153.1542	120.3713	165.1397	149.2355	106.5787	138.8959

Table 6: The average values of `Low` for the different values of `Interval` and `rs`

Interval	rs = -2	rs = -1	rs = 0	rs = 1	rs = 2	Mean
1	728.025	710.504	719.469	744.942	755.798	731.7476
2	357.28	339.793	351.47	367.603	359.252	355.0796
3	230.907	228.604	227.799	238.372	237.315	232.5994
4	171.503	169.7	168.48	174.313	175.201	171.8394
5	135.473	129.022	133.545	138.962	138.87	135.1744
6	111.746	110.873	112.076	113.963	112.493	112.2302
7	91.992	90.91	92.22	96.119	95.609	93.37
8	81.444	79.935	79.718	82.498	84.117	81.5424
9	70.86	68.834	71.446	74.894	71.167	71.4402
10	63.437	61.482	64.39	64.658	64.101	63.6136

Table 7: The average values of `Medium` for the different values of `Interval` and `rs`

Interval	rs = -2	rs = -1	rs = 0	rs = 1	rs = 2	Mean
1	47.248	49.581	46.561	47.412	41.112	46.3828
2	26.548	33.856	28.329	26.149	32.015	29.3794
3	22.706	20.597	23.02	21.656	21.945	21.9848
4	18.976	17.463	18.047	21.075	18.276	18.7674
5	16.522	18.421	15.321	15.574	14.906	16.1488
6	13.209	12.428	11.907	13.971	14.899	13.2828
7	14.172	13.691	13.038	12.9	13.855	13.5312
8	11.917	11.012	11.911	13.1	10.683	11.7246
9	11.95	11.654	10.129	9.591	11.582	10.9812
10	11.128	10.543	9.048	10.527	10.561	10.3614

Table 8: The average values of `High` for the different values of `Interval` and `rs`

Interval	rs = -2	rs = -1	rs = 0	rs = 1	rs = 2	Mean
1	6.163	6.636	5.825	6.437	5.162	6.0446
2	4.418	5.605	4.91	4.118	5.107	4.8316
3	4.611	4.25	4.762	4.818	4.731	4.6344
4	3.973	3.662	4.311	4.391	3.975	4.0624
5	3.784	4.395	4.12	3.849	3.571	3.9438

Table 8: cont....

6	3.878	3.419	3.359	3.598	4.006	3.652
7	4.279	4.022	3.838	3.512	3.992	3.9286
8	3.541	3.588	3.624	3.816	3.223	3.5584
9	3.467	3.723	3.178	3.037	3.524	3.3858
10	3.721	3.215	3.076	3.483	3.728	3.4446

Table 9: The average values of `AvgVisionLow` for the different values of `Interval` and `rs`

Interval	rs = -2	rs = -1	rs = 0	rs = 1	rs = 2	Mean
1	9.987432	9.991743	10.05341	9.991792	10.18732	10.04234
2	9.736038	9.636664	9.714163	9.766573	9.753294	9.721347
3	9.565572	9.575397	9.602995	9.56752	9.646553	9.591607
4	9.509409	9.51356	9.478609	9.533032	9.594813	9.525884
5	9.558859	9.419783	9.448607	9.567634	9.46854	9.492685
6	9.437265	9.540299	9.590996	9.393068	9.435319	9.479389
7	9.328669	9.353625	9.35134	9.431913	9.47204	9.387517
8	9.301396	9.505579	9.240595	9.325895	9.391447	9.352983
9	9.214934	9.200703	9.380852	9.399738	9.317271	9.3027
10	9.243957	9.445001	9.383003	9.293832	9.302026	9.333563

Table 10: The average values of `AvgVisionMedium` for the different values of `Interval` and `rs`

Interval	rs = -2	rs = -1	rs = 0	rs = 1	rs = 2	Mean
1	12.74149	12.75078	12.55186	12.76634	12.89568	12.74123
2	12.52465	12.43942	12.28774	12.08251	12.66054	12.39897
3	12.1049	12.42029	12.20365	12.17875	12.48065	12.27765
4	12.33762	12.39945	12.43831	12.22448	12.33723	12.34742
5	12.25072	12.12252	12.08944	12.22827	12.31285	12.20076
6	12.15186	12.37196	12.11332	11.99983	12.24151	12.1757
7	12.01958	12.12052	12.11346	12.05684	12.28727	12.11953
8	11.99177	12.19301	12.1573	12.24442	11.90578	12.09846
9	12.0123	12.10154	12.21496	12.1497	12.23202	12.1421
10	11.98929	12.14384	12.21496	11.93538	12.37705	12.1321

Table 11: The average values of `AvgVisionHigh` for the different values of `Interval` and `rs`

Interval	rs = -2	rs = -1	rs = 0	rs = 1	rs = 2	Mean
1	13.04435	12.91835	12.73002	12.89084	13.09054	12.93482
2	13.20501	12.68308	12.64043	12.88365	13.00032	12.8825
3	12.47863	12.68756	12.54239	12.65826	12.86036	12.64544
4	12.53353	12.59018	12.66551	12.64999	12.82136	12.65211
5	12.53571	12.41737	12.1456	12.56704	12.61027	12.4552
6	12.41558	12.85264	12.74257	12.70718	12.21098	12.58579
7	12.22521	12.29595	12.41129	12.33239	12.76163	12.4053
8	12.61187	12.37464	12.17355	12.55358	11.91875	12.32648
9	11.8651	12.57369	12.47994	12.33464	12.40579	12.33183
10	12.24598	12.89595	12.82727	11.97806	12.69351	12.52815

Table 12: The average values of `WealthLow` for the different values of `Interval` and `rs`

Interval	rs = -2	rs = -1	rs = 0	rs = 1	rs = 2	Mean
1	119.6962	86.59123	117.2026	108.0563	73.40852	100.991
2	120.1582	84.893	114.3733	103.3917	69.67013	98.49728
3	118.167	85.48324	114.3294	98.82969	68.42653	97.04718
4	109.2902	79.80239	109.9113	94.85133	69.66406	92.70385
5	109.4564	79.93303	111.5244	96.32959	72.84966	94.01862
6	113.4694	78.75559	109.1862	99.95714	68.97528	94.06873
7	112.0539	74.07375	111.3982	109.2675	62.75566	93.9098
8	108.9283	85.22894	103.041	95.737	71.37285	92.86163
9	99.29858	76.84634	102.706	106.4545	63.01349	89.66378
10	97.92527	76.3006	108.63	95.93455	67.84021	89.32612

Table 13: The average values of `WealthMedium` for the different values of `Interval` and `rs`

Interval	rs = -2	rs = -1	rs = 0	rs = 1	rs = 2	Mean
1	470.9242	339.7715	455.6328	429.8219	299.8547	399.201
2	494.8751	325.5702	458.462	429.1111	273.631	396.3299
3	487.9795	347.0585	455.5805	419.3755	273.2604	396.6509
4	435.8457	325.961	445.5315	363.0482	282.815	370.6403
5	437.9444	309.0516	452.1649	383.7461	287.6831	374.118
6	454.3237	312.8964	451.4044	401.5388	265.5936	377.1514
7	432.3156	278.0123	436.1003	416.9055	238.7343	360.4136
8	435.7243	347.7616	393.2428	351.1823	269.1719	359.4166
9	373.8253	286.0343	402.4659	423.0823	232.3604	343.5537
10	362.0379	292.9987	408.5444	339.9388	251.8414	331.0722

Table 14: The average values of `WealthHigh` for the different values of `Interval` and `rs`

Interval	rs = -2	rs = -1	rs = 0	rs = 1	rs = 2	Mean
1	918.2158	678.6968	896.7725	841.6682	601.0073	787.2721
2	980.4998	631.9581	913.7079	857.6578	537.2135	784.2074
3	1004.514	678.3076	895.8054	828.9564	556.6072	792.8381
4	913.8399	657.4855	881.7734	723.6608	571.3476	749.6214
5	902.8804	591.2143	898.1479	758.9375	593.6099	748.958
6	899.2484	627.1582	914.7196	803.6506	560.3977	761.0349
7	866.8715	545.2847	866.3091	838.9747	474.8628	718.4606
8	862.7524	679.5053	755.5552	691.4595	549.3481	707.7241
9	747.2	556.1726	798.7985	865.608	460.0171	685.5592
10	733.1841	576.9057	841.9909	688.5974	498.9822	667.9321

Based on data from Tables 2-14, we generated (Figs. 6 and 9). These figures shows us the evolution of average values of `NoTurtles`, `Women`, `Men`, `MeanGlobalWealth` in function of `Interval` ranging from 1 to 10.

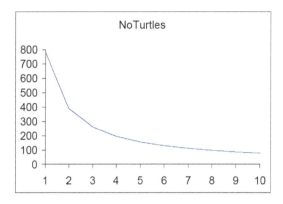

Figure 6: The evolution of average value of `NoTurtles` in function of `Interval`

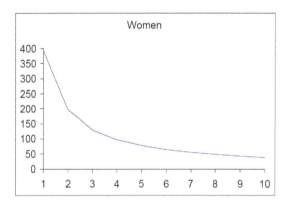

Figure 7: The evolution of average value of `Women` in function of `Interval`

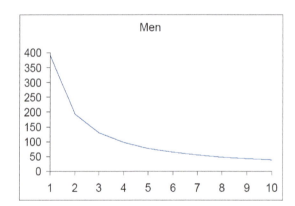

Figure 8: The evolution of average value of `Men` in function of `Interval`

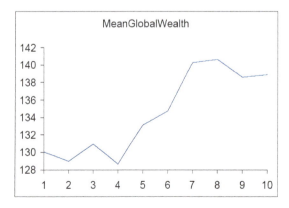

Figure 9: The evolution of average value of `MeanGlobalWealth` in function of `Interval`

THE RESULTS OF COMPUTER EXPERIMENTS IN THE CASE WHEN RESOURCES ARE NONRENEWABLE

The sixth computer experiment is dealing with the case when resources are nonrenewable. Based on data obtained after running this experiment - see Appendix 1, we computed a new set of data that contain average values for the variables NoTurtles, Women, Men, MeanGlobalWealth, Low, Medium, High, AvgVisionLow, AvgVisionMedium, AvgVisionHigh, WealthLow, WealthMedium, and WealthHigh – see Appendix 2 for the evolution in time of these variables and Table **15** for the average values in the case when resources are nonrenewable.

Table 15: The average values of NoTurtles, Women, Men, MeanGlobalWealth, Low, Medium, High, AvgVisionLow, AvgVisionMedium, AvgVisionHigh, WealthLow, WealthMedium, and WealthHigh for the different values of rs

Variable	rs = -2	rs = -1	rs = 0	rs = 1	rs = 2	Mean
NoTurtles	14.07407	17.69388	13.21311	13.30769	10.63291	10.76435
Women	6.981481	9.877551	5.327869	5.892308	4.620253	4.911392
Men	7.092593	7.816327	7.885246	7.415385	6.012658	5.852954
MeanGlobalWealth	73.77747	56.15059	105.1678	81.74986	77.49917	89.2372
Low	8.055556	10.38776	8.57377	7.061538	5.911392	6.1
Medium	3.462963	4.142857	3.065574	3.230769	2.518987	2.512869
High	2.555556	3.163265	1.57377	3.015385	2.202532	2.151477
AvgVisionLow	7.739803	8.355376	8.676476	9.078501	10.77027	10.05379
AvgVisionMedium	8.823967	11.69904	10.67486	11.08269	12.54846	11.73395
AvgVisionHigh	11.53704	13.56599	14.49399	11.04037	11.97257	12.36432
WealthLow	31.89386	21.68127	31.64178	25.40933	23.31974	24.64314
WealthMedium	74.87996	68.37615	106.4235	61.97047	64.23861	68.25164
WealthHigh	128.8745	122.2125	228.9922	124.9572	139.1829	145.3071

REFERENCES

[1]   Sacks J, Welch WJ, Mitchell TJ, Wynn HP, Wynn HP. Design and Analysis of Computer Experiments. Statistical Science. 1989 4(4): 433-35.

[2]   Sieburg HB. Physiological Studies in silico. Studies in the Sciences of Complexity. 1990 12: 321-42.

[3]   Santner TJ, Williams BJ, Notz WI. The Design and Analysis of Computer Experiments. Berlin: Springer; 2003.

[4]   Reese CS, Wilson AG, Hamada M, Martz HF, Ryan KJ. Integrated analysis of computer and physical experiments. Technometrics. 2004 46: 153-64.

[5]   Kennedy MC, O'Hagan A. Predicting the output from a complex computer code when fast approximations are available. Biometrika. 2000 87: 1-13.

[6]   Law AM, Kelton WD. Simulation modeling and analysis. 2nd ed. New York: McGraw-Hill; 1991.

[7]   Kelton WD., Sadowski RP, Sadowski DA. Simulation with Arena - 2nd edition. New York: McGraw-Hill; 2002.

[8]   Banks J, Carson JS, Nelson BL. Discrete event system simulation. 2d ed. Upper Saddle River, N.J.: Prentice-Hall; 1996.

[9]   Kleijnen JPC. Experimental design for sensitivity analysis, optimization, and validation of simulation models. In Banks J (ed.). Handbook of simulation, New York: John Wiley; 1998: 173–223.

[10]   Hood SJ, Welch PD. Experimental design issues in simulation with examples from semiconductor manufacturing. In Swain JJ, Goldsman D, Crain RC, and Wilson JR (ed.). Proceedings of the 1992 Winter Simulation Conference. WSC Board of Directors; 1992: 255–63.

[11]   Swain JJ, Farrington PA. Designing simulation experiments for evaluating manufacturing systems. In Tew JD, Manivannan MS, Sadowski DA, Seila AF. (ed.) Proceedings of the 1994 Winter Simulation Conference. WSC Board of Directors; 1994: 69–76.

[12]   Kelton WD. Statistical analysis of simulation output. In Andradóttir S, Healy KJ, Withers DH, Nelson BL (eds.). Proceedings of the 1997 Winter Simulation Conference. WSC Board of Directors; 1997: 23–30.

CHAPTER 5

CONCLUSIONS

Abstract: In this chapter, we draw the conclusions regarding the evolution of Agent-based Artificial Society described in Chapter 2, implemented in Chapter 3 using NetLogo, and used for a set of computational experiments in Chapter 4.

Based on results obtained after running the six computational experiments done in Chapter 4, we can conclude the following:

(a) When resources are renewable, we have the next conclusions:

    (i)   The evolution of average number of turtles (NoTurtles) is decreasing when the value of the value of resources growth interval (Interval) is increasing;

    (ii)   The same evolution is encountered by the average number of female and male turtles (Women, and Men);

    (iii)   The evolution of average value of global wealth (MeanGlobalWealth) is maintaining relatively steady in the interval [128, 142] as Table 5 of Chapter 4 shows us;

    (iv)   The proportion of turtles from low social class (Low) in the total number of turtles (NoTurtles) is maintaining at a level of about 80-90 percent value as we can see in Table 6 of Chapter 4;

    (v)   The proportion of turtles from medium social class (Medium) in the total number of turtles (NoTurtles) is maintaining at a level of about 5-15 percent value as we can see in Table 7 Chapter 4;

    (vi)   The proportion of turtles from high social class (High) in the total number of turtles (NoTurtles) is maintaining at a level of about 0.5-5 percent value as we can see in Table 8 of Chapter 4;

    (vii)   The average vision of turtles from low class is varying in the interval 9-10, the average vision of turtles from middle class is about 12, and the average vision of turtles from high class is a little higher in comparison with the value obtained for middle social class;

    (viii)   The wealth of turtles from low social class is in the interval 90-100, the wealth of turtles from medium social class is in the interval 300-400, and the wealth of turtles from high class is in the interval 600-700.

(b) When resources are nonrenewable, we draw the next conclusions:

    (i)   In all five runs when resources were nonrenewable the population of turtles did not managed to survive to 1000 years like in the case when resources were renewable;

    (ii)   The maximum period of survive was 78 years, and the minimal period was 48 years;

    (iii)   As Figure 1 of Appendix 3 shows us, the evolution of number of turtles reached a maximum in the interval 30-40 in the period of years 10-15 and after this period of time the population of turtles dropped dramatically to zero level in the next 30 to 60 years;

    (iv)   The average value of global wealth was about 90, as Table 11 of Chapter 4 shows us, that is lower in comparison with the case when resources were renewable;

    (v)   The proportion of turtles from low social class (Low) in the total number of turtles (NoTurtles) is about 57 percent value as we can see in Table 11 of Chapter 4;

    (vi)   The proportion of turtles from medium social class (Medium) in the total number of turtles (NoTurtles) is about 23 percent value as we can see in Table 11 of Chapter 4;

    (vii)   The proportion of turtles from high social class (High) in the total number of turtles (NoTurtles) is about 20 percent value as we can see in Table 11 of Chapter 4;

    (ix)   The average vision of turtles from low class is about 10, the average vision of turtles from middle class is about 12, and the average vision of turtles from high class is a little higher in comparison with the value obtained for middle social class;

Romulus-Catalin Damaceanu (Ed)

(viii) The wealth of turtles from low social class is about 24, the wealth of turtles from medium social class is about 70, and the wealth of turtles from high class is about 150.

As general conclusion, we can say that the results confirm the familiar saying "The rich get richer and the poor get poorer". The computational experiments done in the frame of this book expresses the inequity in the distribution of wealth. Once again we confirm Pareto's law, in which there are a large number of "poor" people, fewer "middle class" people, and many fewer "rich" people.

APPENDIX 1

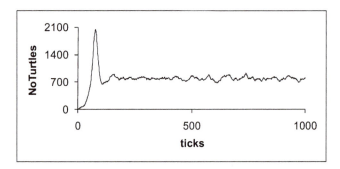

Figure 1: The evolution of turtles' population (NoTurtles) in the case of computer experiment E1 run 1

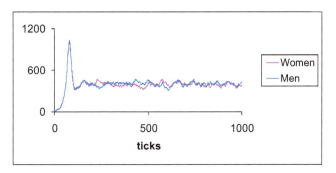

Figure 2: The evolution of female and male turtles (Women, and Men variables) in the case of computer experiment E1 run 1

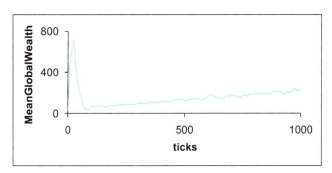

Figure 3: The evolution of average global wealth MeanGlobalWealth in the case of computer experiment E1 run 1

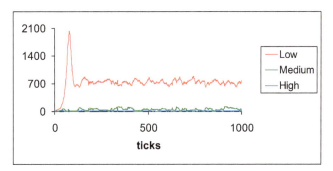

Figure 4: The evolution of number of turtles from low, medium and high class (Low, Medium, High) in the case of computer experiment E1 run 1

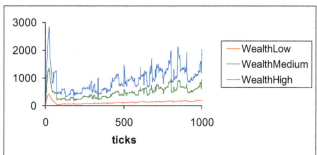

Figure 5: The evolution of global wealth of turtles from low, medium and high class (WealthLow, WealthMedium, WealthHigh) in the case of computer experiment E1 run 1

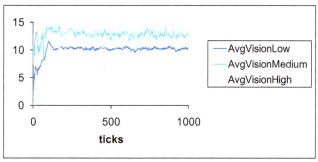

Figure 6: The evolution of turtles vision from low, medium and high class (AvgVisionLow, AvgVisionMedium, AvgVisionHigh) in the case of computer experiment E1 run 1

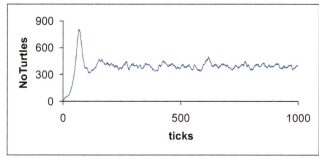

Figure 7: The evolution of turtles' population (NoTurtles) in the case of computer experiment E1 run 2

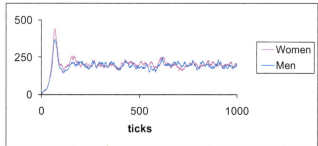

Figure 8: The evolution of female and male turtles (Women, and Men variables) in the case of computer experiment E1 run 2

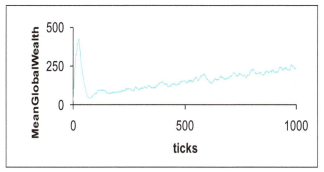

Figure 9: The evolution of average global wealth `MeanGlobalWealth` in the case of computer experiment `E1 run 2`

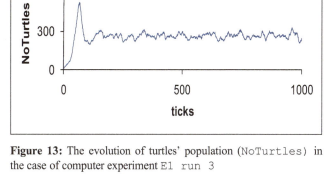

Figure 13: The evolution of turtles' population (`NoTurtles`) in the case of computer experiment `E1 run 3`

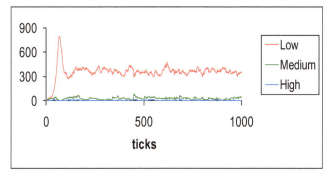

Figure 10: The evolution of number of turtles from low, medium and high class (`Low, Medium, High`) in the case of computer experiment `E1 run 2`

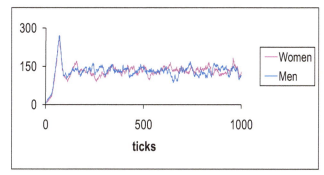

Figure 14: The evolution of female and male turtles (`Women`, and `Men` variables) in the case of computer experiment `E1 run 3`

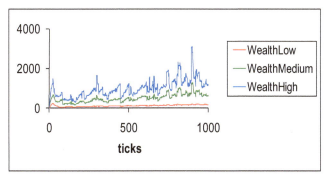

Figure 11: The evolution of global wealth of turtles from low, medium and high class (`WealthLow, WealthMedium, WealthHigh`) in the case of computer experiment `E1 run 2`

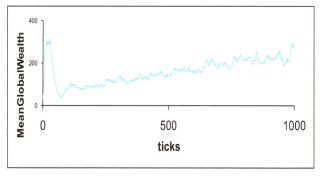

Figure 15: The evolution of average global wealth `MeanGlobalWealth` in the case of computer experiment `E1 run 3`

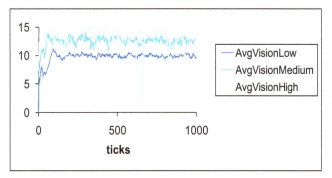

Figure 12: The evolution of turtles vision from low, medium and high class (`AvgVisionLow, AvgVisionMedium, AvgVisionHigh`) in the case of `E1` computer experiment `run 2`

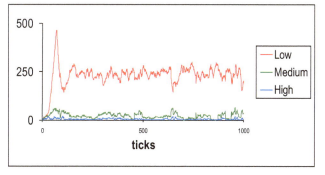

Figure 16: The evolution of number of turtles from low, medium and high class (`Low, Medium, High`) in the case of computer experiment `E1 run 3`

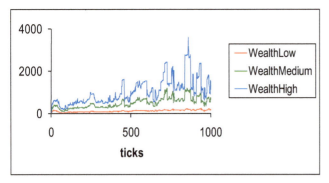

Figure 17: The evolution of global wealth of turtles from low, medium and high class (WealthLow, WealthMedium, WealthHigh) in the case of computer experiment E1 run 3

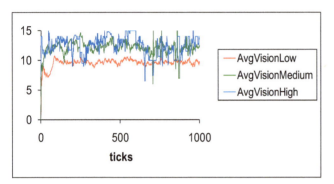

Figure 18: The evolution of turtles vision from low, medium and high class (AvgVisionLow, AvgVisionMedium, AvgVisionHigh) in the case of E1 computer experiment run 3

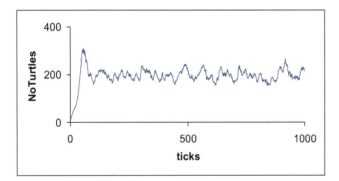

Figure 19: The evolution of turtles' population (NoTurtles) in the case of computer experiment E1 run 4

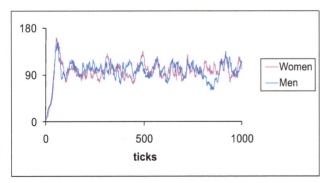

Figure 20: The evolution of female and male turtles (Women, and Men variables) in the case of computer experiment E1 run 4

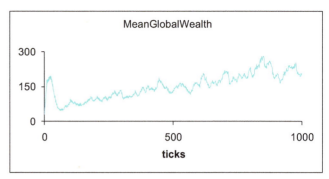

Figure 21: The evolution of average global wealth MeanGlobalWealth in the case of computer experiment E1 run 4

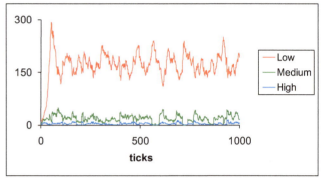

Figure 22: The evolution of number of turtles from low, medium and high class (Low, Medium, High) in the case of computer experiment E1 run 4

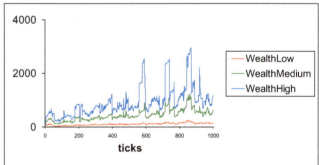

Figure 23: The evolution of global wealth of turtles from low, medium and high class (WealthLow, WealthMedium, WealthHigh) in the case of computer experiment E1 run 4

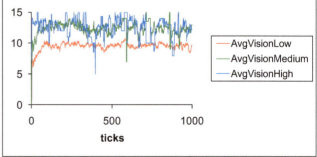

Figure 24: The evolution of turtles vision from low, medium and high class (AvgVisionLow, AvgVisionMedium, AvgVisionHigh) in the case of E1 computer experiment run 4

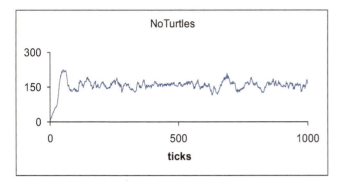

Figure 25: The evolution of turtles' population (`NoTurtles`) in the case of computer experiment `E1 run 5`

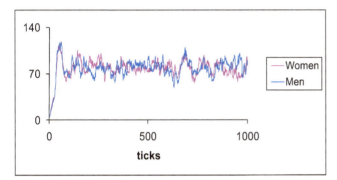

Figure 26: The evolution of female and male turtles (`Women`, and `Men` variables) in the case of computer experiment `E1 run 5`

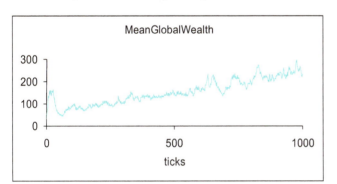

Figure 27: The evolution of average global wealth `MeanGlobalWealth` in the case of computer experiment `E1 run 5`

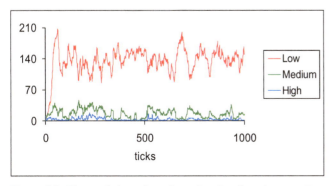

Figure 28: The evolution of number of turtles from low, medium and high class (`Low`, `Medium`, `High`) in the case of computer experiment `E1 run 5`

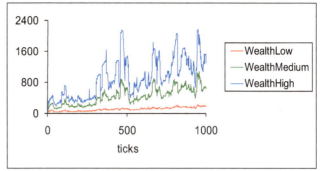

Figure 29: The evolution of global wealth of turtles from low, medium and high class (`WealthLow`, `WealthMedium`, `WealthHigh`) in the case of computer experiment `E1 run 5`

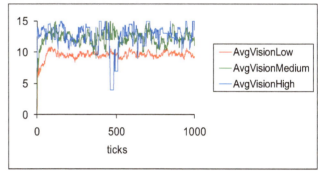

Figure 30: The evolution of turtles vision from low, medium and high class (`AvgVisionLow`, `AvgVisionMedium`, `AvgVisionHigh`) in the case of `E1` computer experiment `run 5`

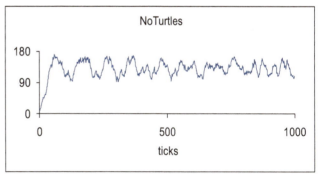

Figure 31: The evolution of turtles' population (`NoTurtles`) in the case of computer experiment `E1 run 6`

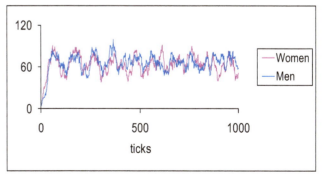

Figure 32: The evolution of female and male turtles (`Women`, and `Men` variables) in the case of computer experiment `E1 run 6`

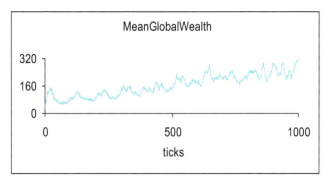

Figure 33: The evolution of average global wealth `MeanGlobalWealth` in the case of computer experiment `E1 run 6`

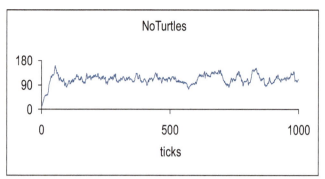

Figure 37: The evolution of turtles' population (`NoTurtles`) in the case of computer experiment `E1 run 7`

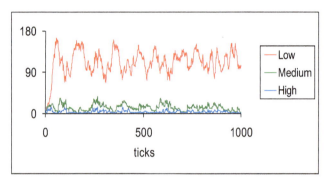

Figure 34: The evolution of number of turtles from low, medium and high class (`Low`, `Medium`, `High`) in the case of computer experiment `E1 run 6`

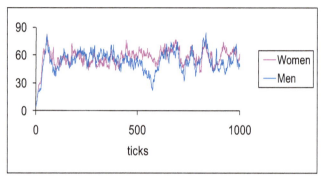

Figure 38: The evolution of female and male turtles (`Women`, and `Men` variables) in the case of computer experiment `E1 run 7`

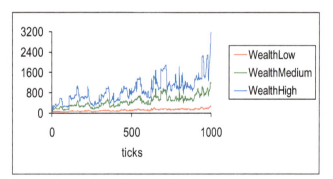

Figure 35: The evolution of global wealth of turtles from low, medium and high class (`WealthLow`, `WealthMedium`, `WealthHigh`) in the case of computer experiment `E1 run 6`

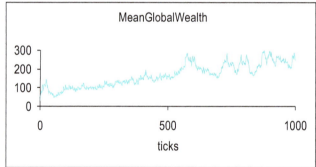

Figure 39: The evolution of average global wealth `MeanGlobalWealth` in the case of computer experiment `E1 run 7`

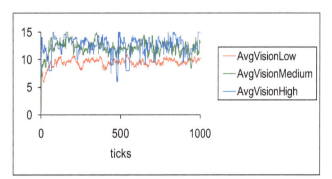

Figure 36: The evolution of turtles vision from low, medium and high class (`AvgVisionLow`, `AvgVisionMedium`, `AvgVisionHigh`) in the case of `E1` computer experiment `run 6`

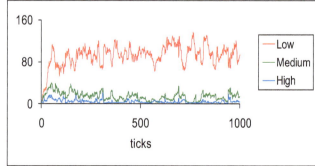

Figure 40: The evolution of number of turtles from low, medium and high class (`Low`, `Medium`, `High`) in the case of computer experiment `E1 run 7`

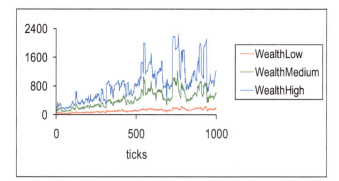

Figure 41: The evolution of global wealth of turtles from low, medium and high class (WealthLow, WealthMedium, WealthHigh) in the case of computer experiment E1 run 7

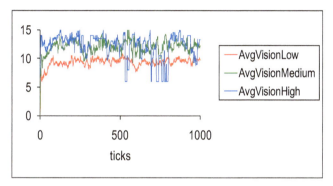

Figure 42: The evolution of turtles vision from low, medium and high class (AvgVisionLow, AvgVisionMedium, AvgVisionHigh) in the case of E1 computer experiment run 7

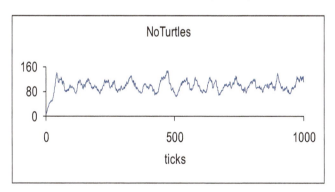

Figure 43: The evolution of turtles' population (NoTurtles) in the case of computer experiment E1 run 8

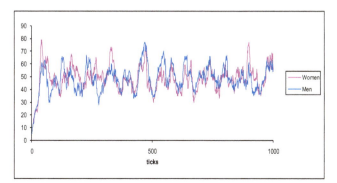

Figure 44: The evolution of female and male turtles (Women, and Men variables) in the case of computer experiment E1 run 8

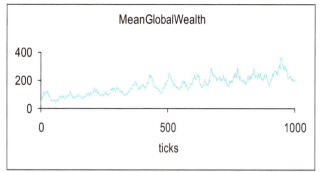

Figure 45: The evolution of average global wealth MeanGlobalWealth in the case of computer experiment E1 run 8

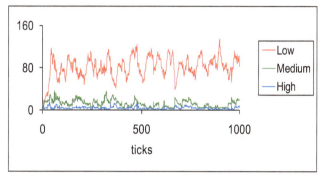

Figure 46: The evolution of number of turtles from low, medium and high class (Low, Medium, High) in the case of computer experiment E1 run 8

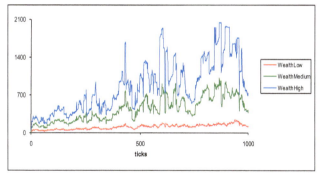

Figure 47: The evolution of global wealth of turtles from low, medium and high class (WealthLow, WealthMedium, WealthHigh) in the case of computer experiment E1 run 8

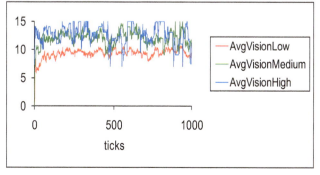

Figure 48: The evolution of turtles vision from low, medium and high class (AvgVisionLow, AvgVisionMedium, AvgVisionHigh) in the case of E1 computer experiment run 8

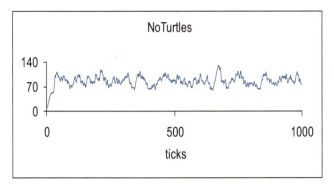

Figure 49: The evolution of turtles' population (NoTurtles) in the case of computer experiment E1 run 9

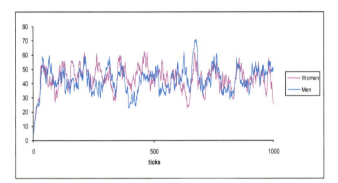

Figure 50: The evolution of female and male turtles (Women, and Men variables) in the case of computer experiment E1 run 9

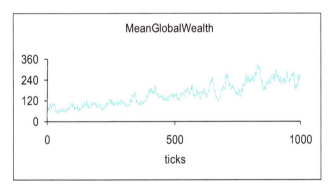

Figure 51: The evolution of average global wealth MeanGlobalWealth in the case of computer experiment E1 run 9

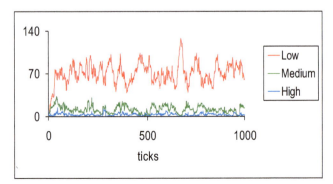

Figure 52: The evolution of number of turtles from low, medium and high class (Low, Medium, High) in the case of computer experiment E1 run 9

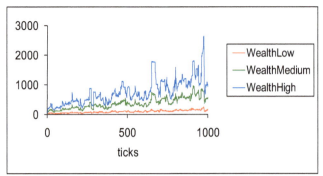

Figure 53: The evolution of global wealth of turtles from low, medium and high class (WealthLow, WealthMedium, WealthHigh) in the case of computer experiment E1 run 9

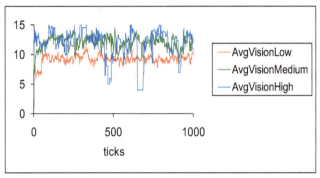

Figure 54: The evolution of turtles vision from low, medium and high class (AvgVisionLow, AvgVisionMedium, AvgVisionHigh) in the case of E1 computer experiment run 9

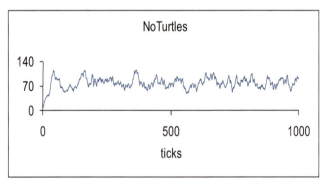

Figure 55: The evolution of turtles' population (NoTurtles) in the case of computer experiment E1 run 10

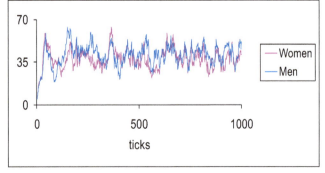

Figure 56: The evolution of female and male turtles (Women, and Men variables) in the case of computer experiment E1 run 10

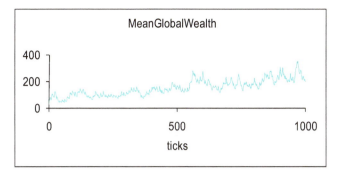

Figure 57: The evolution of average global wealth `MeanGlobalWealth` in the case of computer experiment E1 run 10

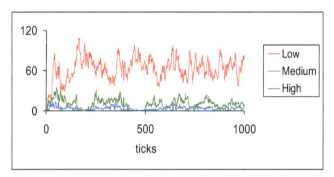

Figure 58: The evolution of number of turtles from low, medium and high class (`Low`, `Medium`, `High`) in the case of computer experiment E1 run 10

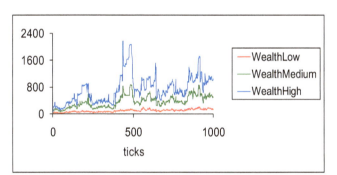

Figure 59: The evolution of global wealth of turtles from low, medium and high class (`WealthLow`, `WealthMedium`, `WealthHigh`) in the case of computer experiment E1 run 10

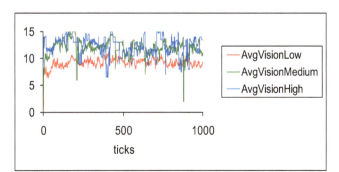

Figure 60: The evolution of turtles vision from low, medium and high class (`AvgVisionLow`, `AvgVisionMedium`, `AvgVisionHigh`) in the case of E1 computer experiment run 10

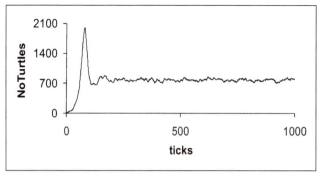

Figure 61: The evolution of turtles' population (`NoTurtles`) in the case of computer experiment E2 run 1

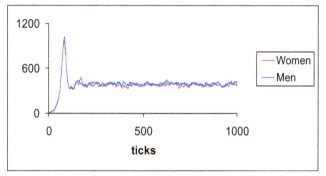

Figure 62: The evolution of female and male turtles (`Women`, and `Men` variables) in the case of computer experiment E2 run 1

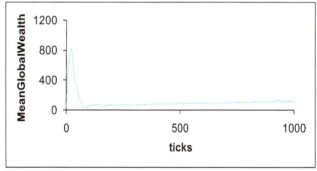

Figure 63: The evolution of average global wealth `MeanGlobalWealth` in the case of computer experiment E2 run 1

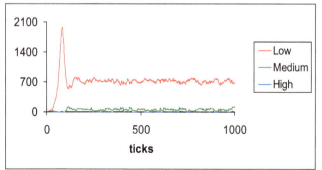

Figure 64: The evolution of number of turtles from low, medium and high class (`Low`, `Medium`, `High`) in the case of computer experiment E2 run 1

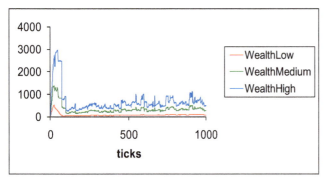

Figure 65: The evolution of global wealth of turtles from low, medium and high class (WealthLow, WealthMedium, WealthHigh) in the case of computer experiment E2 run 1

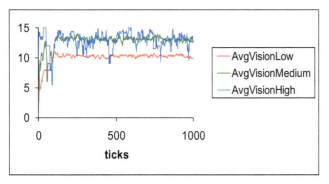

Figure 66: The evolution of turtles vision from low, medium and high class (AvgVisionLow, AvgVisionMedium, AvgVisionHigh) in the case of E2 computer experiment run 1

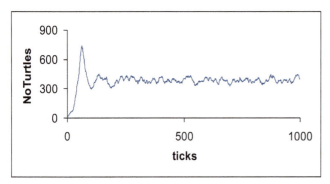

Figure 67: The evolution of turtles' population (NoTurtles) in the case of computer experiment E2 run 2

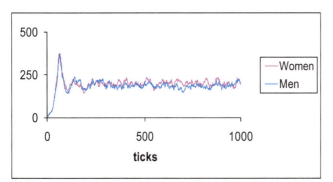

Figure 68: The evolution of female and male turtles (Women, and Men variables) in the case of computer experiment E2 run 2

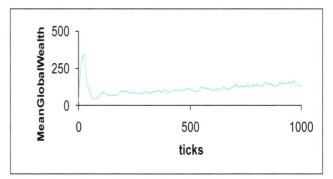

Figure 69: The evolution of average global wealth MeanGlobalWealth in the case of computer experiment E2 run 2

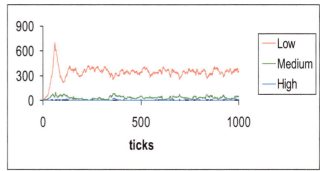

Figure 70: The evolution of number of turtles from low, medium and high class (Low, Medium, High) in the case of computer experiment E2 run 2

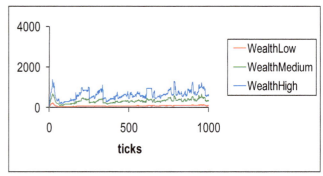

Figure 71: The evolution of global wealth of turtles from low, medium and high class (WealthLow, WealthMedium, WealthHigh) in the case of computer experiment E2 run 2

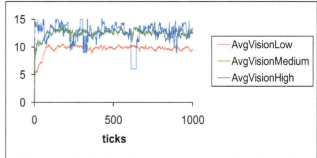

Figure 72: The evolution of turtles vision from low, medium and high class (AvgVisionLow, AvgVisionMedium, AvgVisionHigh) in the case of E2 computer experiment run 2

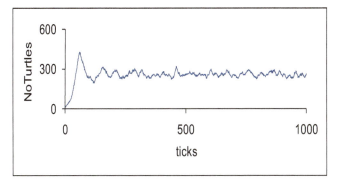

Figure 73: The evolution of turtles' population (NoTurtles) in the case of computer experiment E2 run 3

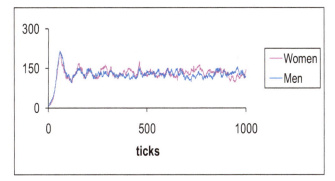

Figure 74: The evolution of female and male turtles (Women, and Men variables) in the case of computer experiment E2 run 3

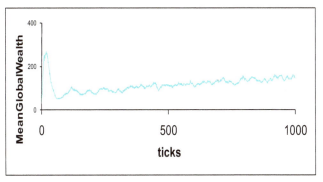

Figure 75: The evolution of average global wealth MeanGlobalWealth in the case of computer experiment E2 run 3

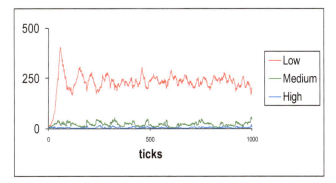

Figure 76: The evolution of number of turtles from low, medium and high class (Low, Medium, High) in the case of computer experiment E2 run 3

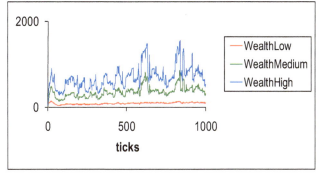

Figure 77: The evolution of global wealth of turtles from low, medium and high class (WealthLow, WealthMedium, WealthHigh) in the case of computer experiment E2 run 3

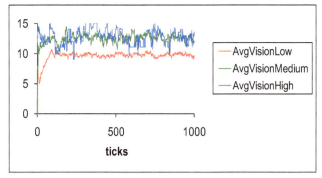

Figure 78: The evolution of turtles vision from low, medium and high class (AvgVisionLow, AvgVisionMedium, AvgVisionHigh) in the case of E2 computer experiment run 3

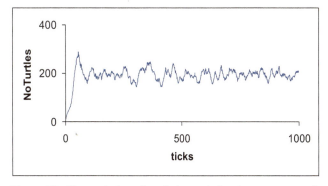

Figure 79: The evolution of turtles' population (NoTurtles) in the case of computer experiment E2 run 4

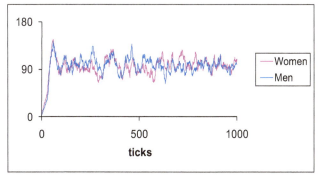

Figure 80: The evolution of female and male turtles (Women, and Men variables) in the case of computer experiment E2 run 4

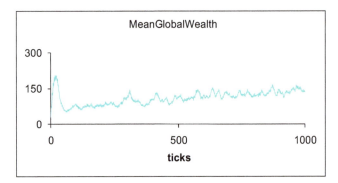

Figure 81: The evolution of average global wealth `MeanGlobalWealth` in the case of computer experiment `E2 run 4`

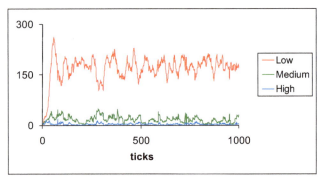

Figure 82: The evolution of number of turtles from low, medium and high class (`Low`, `Medium`, `High`) in the case of computer experiment `E2 run 4`

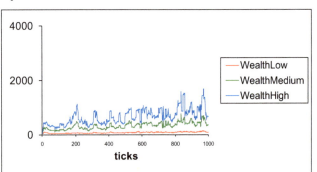

Figure 83: The evolution of global wealth of turtles from low, medium and high class (`WealthLow`, `WealthMedium`, `WealthHigh`) in the case of computer experiment `E2 run 4`

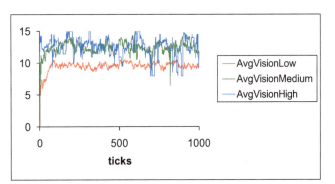

Figure 84: The evolution of turtles vision from low, medium and high class (`AvgVisionLow`, `AvgVisionMedium`, `AvgVisionHigh`) in the case of `E2` computer experiment `run 4`

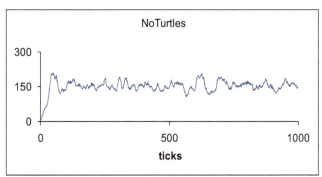

Figure 85: The evolution of turtles' population (`NoTurtles`) in the case of computer experiment `E2 run 5`

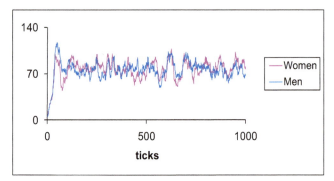

Figure 86: The evolution of female and male turtles (`Women`, and `Men` variables) in the case of computer experiment `E2 run 5`

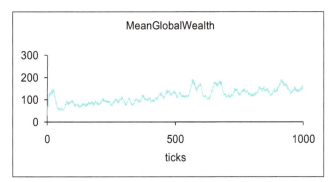

Figure 87: The evolution of average global wealth `MeanGlobalWealth` in the case of computer experiment `E2 run 5`

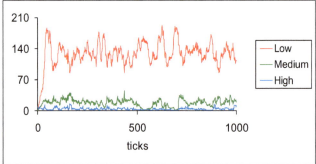

Figure 88: The evolution of number of turtles from low, medium and high class (`Low`, `Medium`, `High`) in the case of computer experiment `E2 run 5`

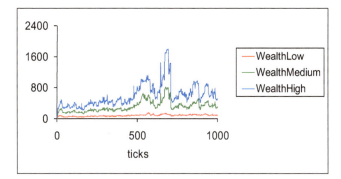

Figure 89: The evolution of global wealth of turtles from low, medium and high class (WealthLow, WealthMedium, WealthHigh) in the case of computer experiment E2 run 5

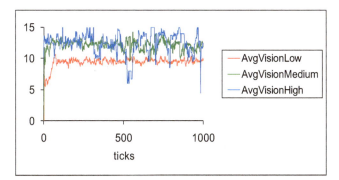

Figure 90: The evolution of turtles vision from low, medium and high class (AvgVisionLow, AvgVisionMedium, AvgVisionHigh) in the case of E2 computer experiment run 5

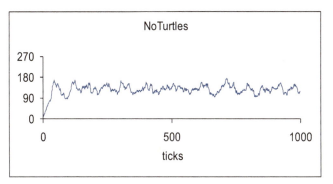

Figure 91: The evolution of turtles' population (NoTurtles) in the case of computer experiment E2 run 6

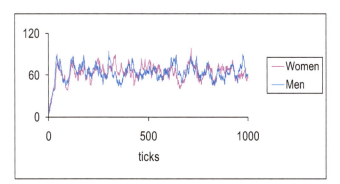

Figure 92: The evolution of female and male turtles (Women, and Men variables) in the case of computer experiment E2 run 6

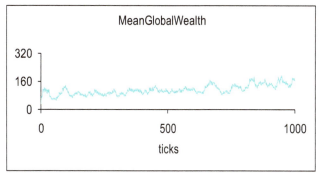

Figure 93: The evolution of average global wealth MeanGlobalWealth in the case of computer experiment E2 run 6

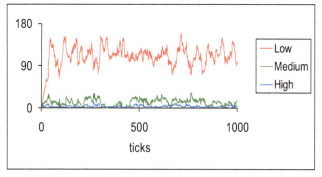

Figure 94: The evolution of number of turtles from low, medium and high class (Low, Medium, High) in the case of computer experiment E2 run 6

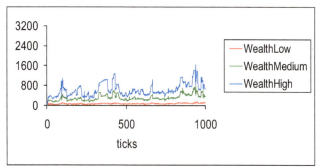

Figure 95: The evolution of global wealth of turtles from low, medium and high class (WealthLow, WealthMedium, WealthHigh) in the case of computer experiment E2 run 6

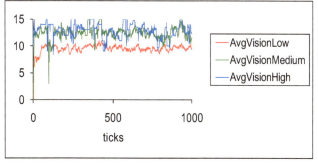

Figure 96: The evolution of turtles vision from low, medium and high class (AvgVisionLow, AvgVisionMedium, AvgVisionHigh) in the case of E2 computer experiment run 6

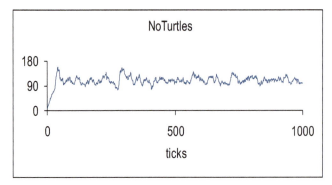

Figure 97: The evolution of turtles' population (NoTurtles) in the case of computer experiment E2 run 7

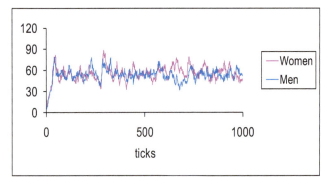

Figure 98: The evolution of female and male turtles (Women, and Men variables) in the case of computer experiment E2 run 7

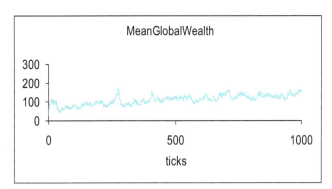

Figure 99: The evolution of average global wealth MeanGlobalWealth in the case of computer experiment E2 run 7

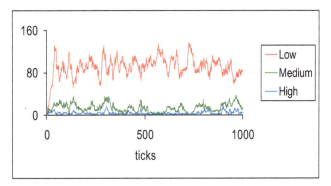

Figure 100: The evolution of number of turtles from low, medium and high class (Low, Medium, High) in the case of computer experiment E2 run 7

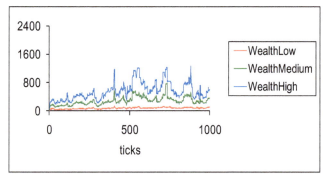

Figure 101: The evolution of global wealth of turtles from low, medium and high class (WealthLow, WealthMedium, WealthHigh) in the case of computer experiment E2 run 7

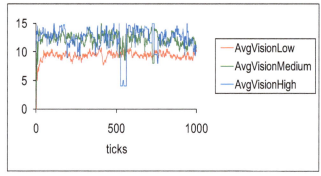

Figure 102: The evolution of turtles vision from low, medium and high class (AvgVisionLow, AvgVisionMedium, AvgVisionHigh) in the case of E2 computer experiment run 7

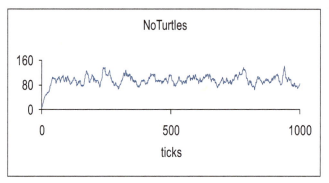

Figure 103: The evolution of turtles' population (NoTurtles) in the case of computer experiment E2 run 8

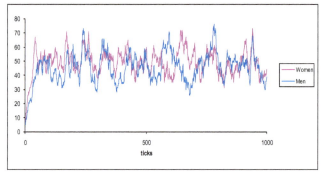

Figure 104: The evolution of female and male turtles (Women, and Men variables) in the case of computer experiment E2 run 8

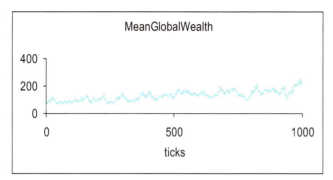

Figure 105: The evolution of average global wealth `MeanGlobalWealth` in the case of computer experiment `E2 run 8`

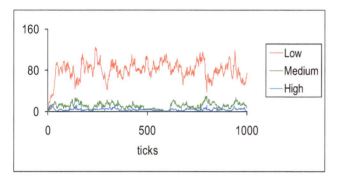

Figure 106: The evolution of number of turtles from low, medium and high class (`Low`, `Medium`, `High`) in the case of computer experiment `E2 run 8`

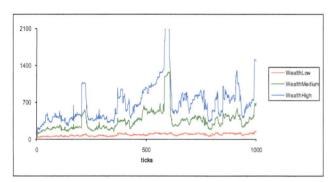

Figure 107: The evolution of global wealth of turtles from low, medium and high class (`WealthLow`, `WealthMedium`, `WealthHigh`) in the case of computer experiment `E2 run 8`

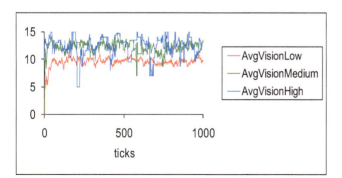

Figure 108: The evolution of turtles vision from low, medium and high class (`AvgVisionLow`, `AvgVisionMedium`, `AvgVisionHigh`) in the case of `E2` computer experiment `run 8`

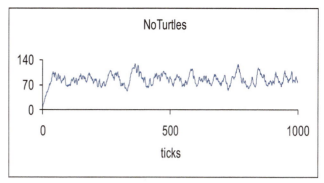

Figure 109: The evolution of turtles' population (`NoTurtles`) in the case of computer experiment `E2 run 9`

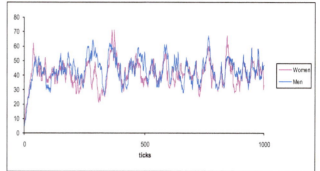

Figure 110: The evolution of female and male turtles (`Women`, and `Men` variables) in the case of computer experiment `E2 run 9`

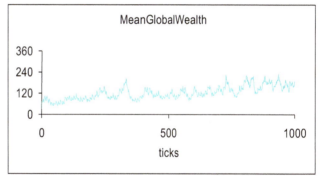

Figure 111: The evolution of average global wealth `MeanGlobalWealth` in the case of computer experiment `E2 run 9`

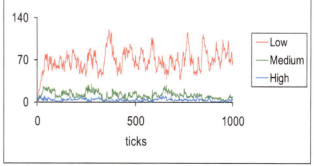

Figure 112: The evolution of number of turtles from low, medium and high class (`Low`, `Medium`, `High`) in the case of computer experiment `E2 run 9`

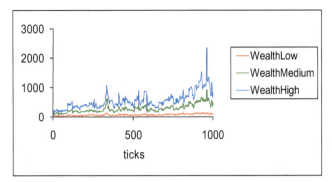

Figure 113: The evolution of global wealth of turtles from low, medium and high class (WealthLow, WealthMedium, WealthHigh) in the case of computer experiment E2 run 9

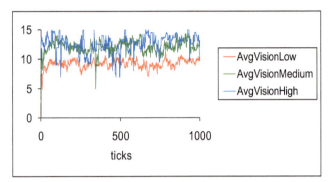

Figure 114: The evolution of turtles vision from low, medium and high class (AvgVisionLow, AvgVisionMedium, AvgVisionHigh) in the case of E2 computer experiment run 9

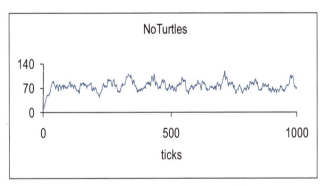

Figure 115: The evolution of turtles' population (NoTurtles) in the case of computer experiment E2 run 10

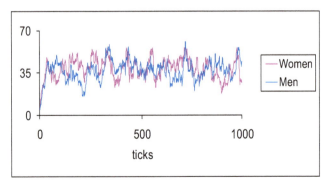

Figure 116: The evolution of female and male turtles (Women, and Men variables) in the case of computer experiment E2 run 10

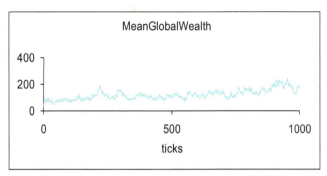

Figure 117: The evolution of average global wealth MeanGlobalWealth in the case of computer experiment E2 run 10

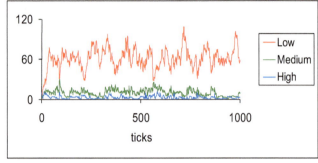

Figure 118: The evolution of number of turtles from low, medium and high class (Low, Medium, High) in the case of computer experiment E2 run 10

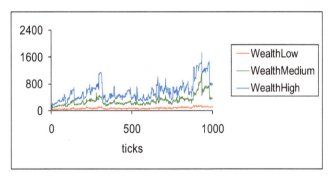

Figure 119: The evolution of global wealth of turtles from low, medium and high class (WealthLow, WealthMedium, WealthHigh) in the case of computer experiment E2 run 10

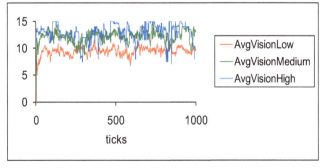

Figure 120: The evolution of turtles vision from low, medium and high class (AvgVisionLow, AvgVisionMedium, AvgVisionHigh) in the case of E2 computer experiment run 10

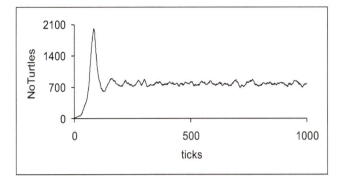

Figure 121: The evolution of turtles' population (`NoTurtles`) in the case of computer experiment `E3 run 1`

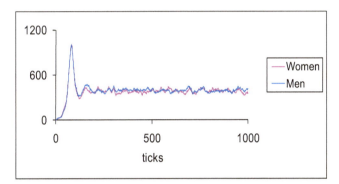

Figure 122: The evolution of female and male turtles (`Women`, and `Men` variables) in the case of computer experiment `E3 run 1`

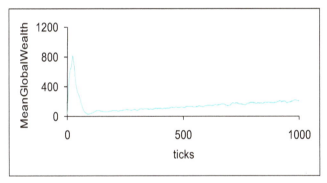

Figure 123: The evolution of average global wealth `MeanGlobalWealth` in the case of computer experiment `E3 run 1`

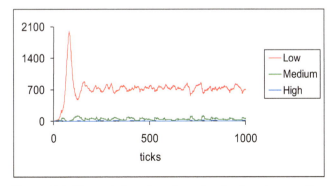

Figure 124: The evolution of number of turtles from low, medium and high class (`Low`, `Medium`, `High`) in the case of computer experiment `E3 run 1`

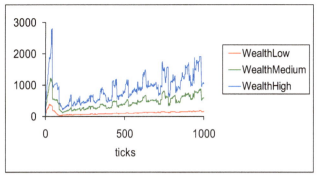

Figure 125: The evolution of global wealth of turtles from low, medium and high class (`WealthLow`, `WealthMedium`, `WealthHigh`) in the case of computer experiment `E3 run 1`

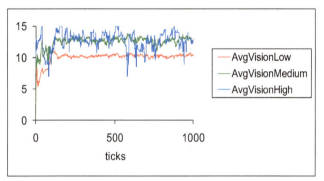

Figure 126: The evolution of turtles vision from low, medium and high class (`AvgVisionLow`, `AvgVisionMedium`, `AvgVisionHigh`) in the case of `E3` computer experiment `run 1`

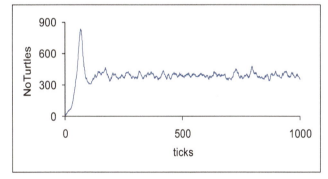

Figure 127: The evolution of turtles' population (`NoTurtles`) in the case of computer experiment `E3 run 2`

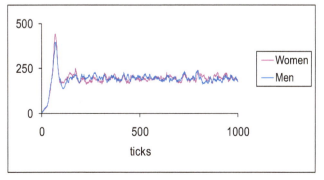

Figure 128: The evolution of female and male turtles (`Women`, and `Men` variables) in the case of computer experiment `E3 run 2`

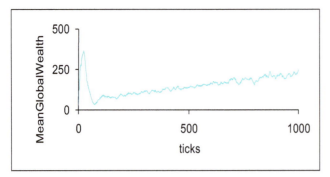

Figure 129: The evolution of average global wealth `MeanGlobalWealth` in the case of computer experiment `E3 run 2`

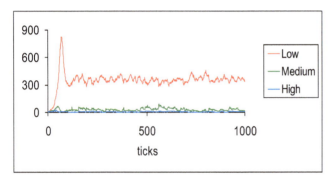

Figure 130: The evolution of number of turtles from low, medium and high class (`Low`, `Medium`, `High`) in the case of computer experiment `E3 run 2`

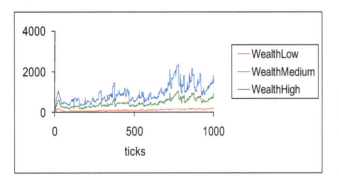

Figure 131: The evolution of global wealth of turtles from low, medium and high class (`WealthLow`, `WealthMedium`, `WealthHigh`) in the case of computer experiment `E3 run 2`

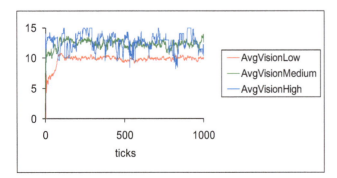

Figure 132: The evolution of turtles vision from low, medium and high class (`AvgVisionLow`, `AvgVisionMedium`, `AvgVisionHigh`) in the case of `E3` computer experiment `run 2`

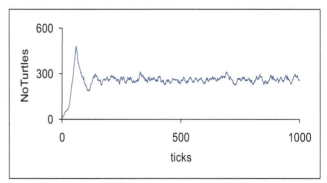

Figure 133: The evolution of turtles' population (`NoTurtles`) in the case of computer experiment `E3 run 3`

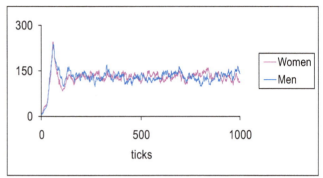

Figure 134: The evolution of female and male turtles (`Women`, and `Men` variables) in the case of computer experiment `E3 run 3`

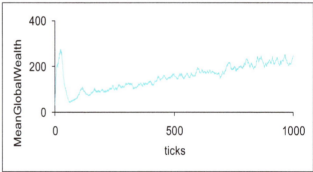

Figure 135: The evolution of average global wealth `MeanGlobalWealth` in the case of computer experiment `E3 run 3`

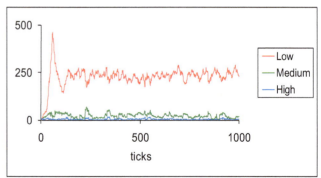

Figure 136: The evolution of number of turtles from low, medium and high class (`Low`, `Medium`, `High`) in the case of computer experiment `E3 run 3`

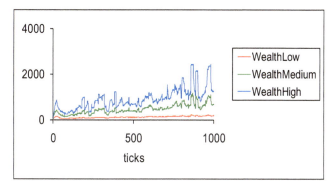

Figure 137: The evolution of global wealth of turtles from low, medium and high class (WealthLow, WealthMedium, WealthHigh) in the case of computer experiment E3 run 3

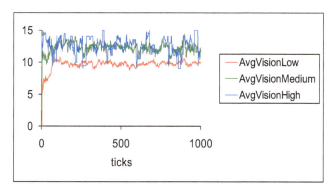

Figure 138: The evolution of turtles vision from low, medium and high class (AvgVisionLow, AvgVisionMedium, AvgVisionHigh) in the case of E3 computer experiment run 3

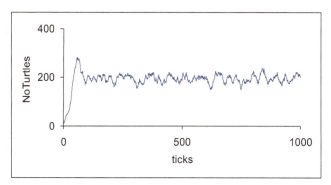

Figure 139: The evolution of turtles' population (NoTurtles) in the case of computer experiment E3 run 4

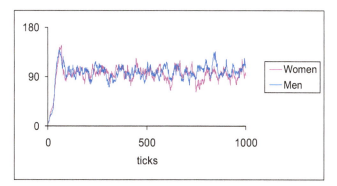

Figure 140: The evolution of female and male turtles (Women, and Men variables) in the case of computer experiment E3 run 4

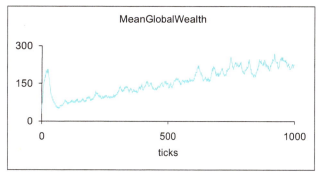

Figure 141: The evolution of average global wealth MeanGlobalWealth in the case of computer experiment E3 run 4

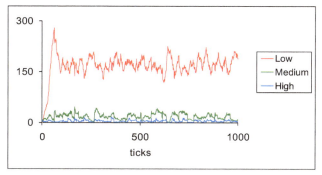

Figure 142: The evolution of number of turtles from low, medium and high class (Low, Medium, High) in the case of computer experiment E3 run 4

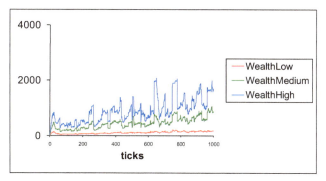

Figure 143: The evolution of global wealth of turtles from low, medium and high class (WealthLow, WealthMedium, WealthHigh) in the case of computer experiment E3 run 4

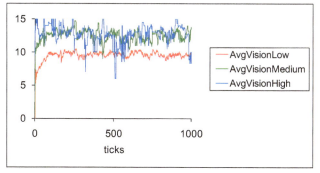

Figure 144: The evolution of turtles vision from low, medium and high class (AvgVisionLow, AvgVisionMedium, AvgVisionHigh) in the case of E3 computer experiment run 4

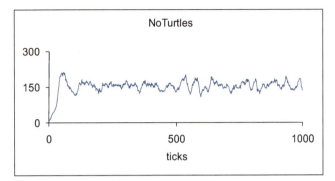

Figure 145: The evolution of turtles' population (NoTurtles) in the case of computer experiment E3 run 5

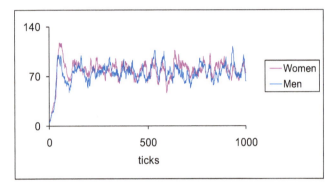

Figure 146: The evolution of female and male turtles (Women, and Men variables) in the case of computer experiment E3 run 5

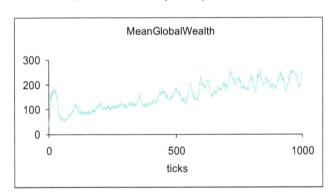

Figure 147: The evolution of average global wealth MeanGlobalWealth in the case of computer experiment E3 run 5

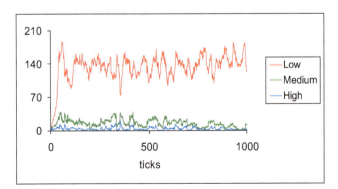

Figure 148: The evolution of number of turtles from low, medium and high class (Low, Medium, High) in the case of computer experiment E3 run 5

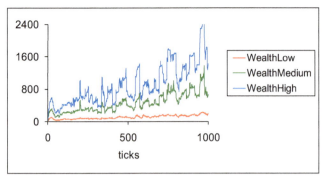

Figure 149: The evolution of global wealth of turtles from low, medium and high class (WealthLow, WealthMedium, WealthHigh) in the case of computer experiment E3 run 5

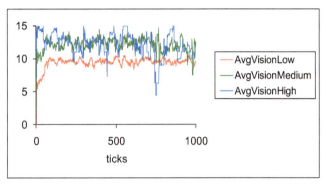

Figure 150: The evolution of turtles vision from low, medium and high class (AvgVisionLow, AvgVisionMedium, AvgVisionHigh) in the case of E3 computer experiment run 5

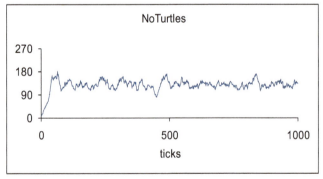

Figure 151: The evolution of turtles' population (NoTurtles) in the case of computer experiment E3 run 6

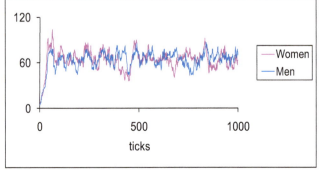

Figure 152: The evolution of female and male turtles (Women, and Men variables) in the case of computer experiment E3 run 6

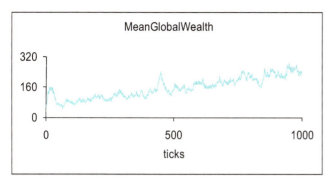

Figure 153: The evolution of average global wealth `MeanGlobalWealth` in the case of computer experiment `E3 run 6`

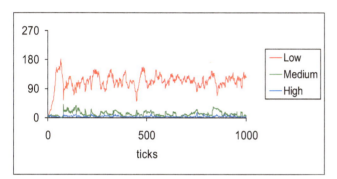

Figure 154: The evolution of number of turtles from low, medium and high class (`Low`, `Medium`, `High`) in the case of computer experiment `E3 run 6`

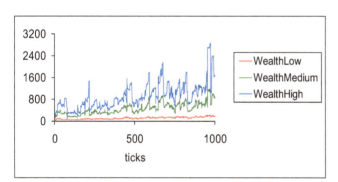

Figure 155: The evolution of global wealth of turtles from low, medium and high class (`WealthLow`, `WealthMedium`, `WealthHigh`) in the case of computer experiment `E3 run 6`

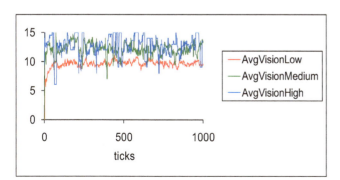

Figure 156: The evolution of turtles vision from low, medium and high class (`AvgVisionLow`, `AvgVisionMedium`, `AvgVisionHigh`) in the case of `E3` computer experiment `run 6`

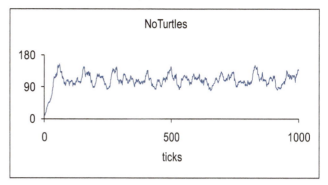

Figure 157: The evolution of turtles' population (`NoTurtles`) in the case of computer experiment `E3 run 7`

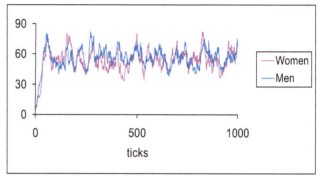

Figure 158: The evolution of female and male turtles (`Women`, and `Men` variables) in the case of computer experiment `E3 run 7`

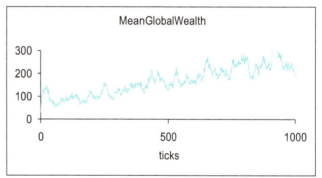

Figure 159: The evolution of average global wealth `MeanGlobalWealth` in the case of computer experiment `E3 run 7`

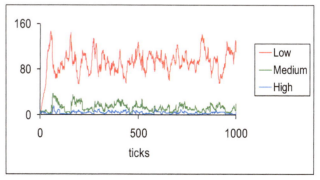

Figure 160: The evolution of number of turtles from low, medium and high class (`Low`, `Medium`, `High`) in the case of computer experiment `E3 run 7`

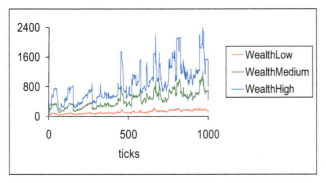

Figure 161: The evolution of global wealth of turtles from low, medium and high class (`WealthLow`, `WealthMedium`, `WealthHigh`) in the case of computer experiment `E3 run 7`

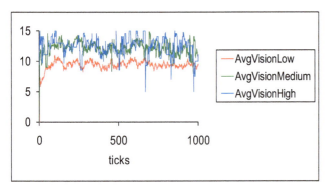

Figure 162: The evolution of turtles vision from low, medium and high class (`AvgVisionLow`, `AvgVisionMedium`, `AvgVisionHigh`) in the case of `E3` computer experiment `run 7`

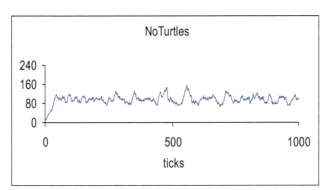

Figure 163: The evolution of turtles' population (`NoTurtles`) in the case of computer experiment `E3 run 8`

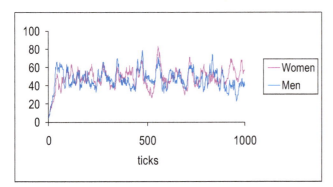

Figure 164: The evolution of female and male turtles (`Women`, and `Men` variables) in the case of computer experiment `E3 run 8`

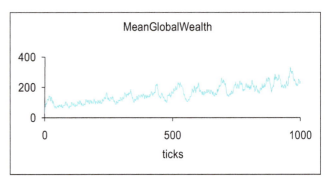

Figure 165: The evolution of average global wealth `MeanGlobalWealth` in the case of computer experiment `E3 run 8`

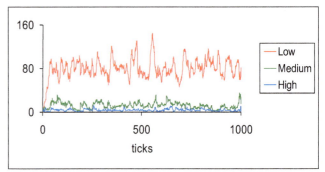

Figure 166: The evolution of number of turtles from low, medium and high class (`Low`, `Medium`, `High`) in the case of computer experiment `E3 run 8`

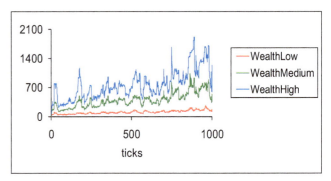

Figure 167: The evolution of global wealth of turtles from low, medium and high class (`WealthLow`, `WealthMedium`, `WealthHigh`) in the case of computer experiment `E3 run 8`

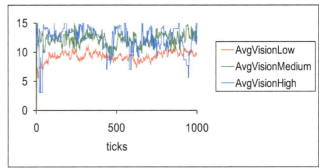

Figure 168: The evolution of turtles vision from low, medium and high class (`AvgVisionLow`, `AvgVisionMedium`, `AvgVisionHigh`) in the case of `E3` computer experiment `run 8`

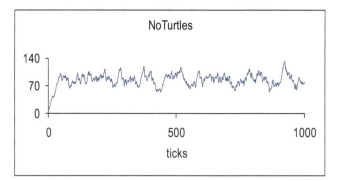

Figure 169: The evolution of turtles' population (NoTurtles) in the case of computer experiment E3 run 9

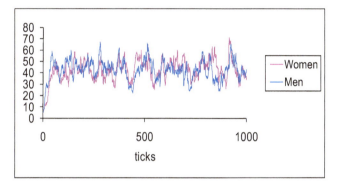

Figure 170: The evolution of female and male turtles (Women, and Men variables) in the case of computer experiment E3 run 9

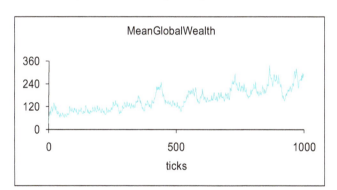

Figure 171: The evolution of average global wealth MeanGlobalWealth in the case of computer experiment E3 run 9

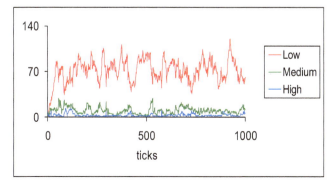

Figure 172: The evolution of number of turtles from low, medium and high class (Low, Medium, High) in the case of computer experiment E3 run 9

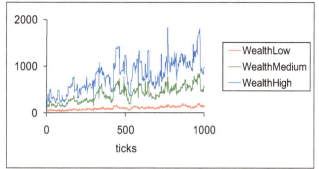

Figure 173: The evolution of global wealth of turtles from low, medium and high class (WealthLow, WealthMedium, WealthHigh) in the case of computer experiment E3 run 9

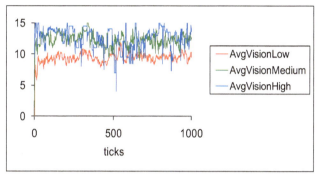

Figure 174: The evolution of turtles vision from low, medium and high class (AvgVisionLow, AvgVisionMedium, AvgVisionHigh) in the case of E3 computer experiment run 9

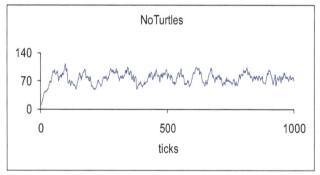

Figure 175: The evolution of turtles' population (NoTurtles) in the case of computer experiment E3 run 10

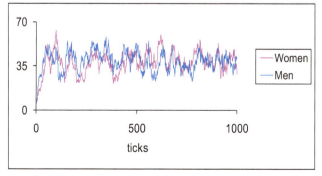

Figure 176: The evolution of female and male turtles (Women, and Men variables) in the case of computer experiment E3 run 10

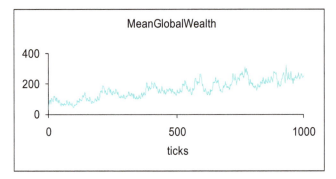

Figure 177: The evolution of average global wealth `MeanGlobalWealth` in the case of computer experiment `E3` `run 10`

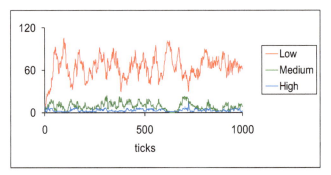

Figure 178: The evolution of number of turtles from low, medium and high class (`Low`, `Medium`, `High`) in the case of computer experiment `E3` `run 10`

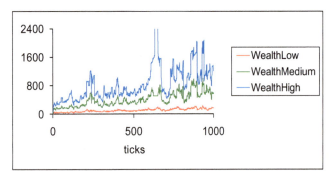

Figure 179: The evolution of global wealth of turtles from low, medium and high class (`WealthLow`, `WealthMedium`, `WealthHigh`) in the case of computer experiment `E3` `run 10`

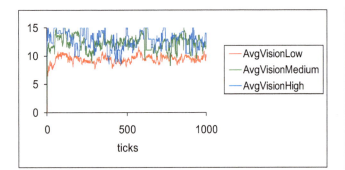

Figure 180: The evolution of turtles vision from low, medium and high class (`AvgVisionLow`, `AvgVisionMedium`, `AvgVisionHigh`) in the case of `E3` computer experiment `run 10`

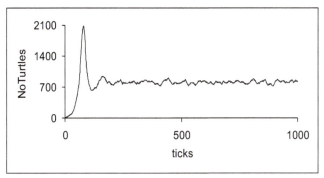

Figure 181: The evolution of turtles' population (`NoTurtles`) in the case of computer experiment `E4` `run 1`

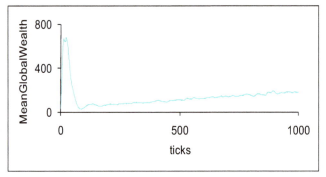

Figure 182: The evolution of female and male turtles (`Women`, and `Men` variables) in the case of computer experiment `E4` `run 1`

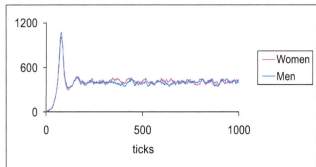

Figure 183: The evolution of average global wealth `MeanGlobalWealth` in the case of computer experiment `E4` `run 1`

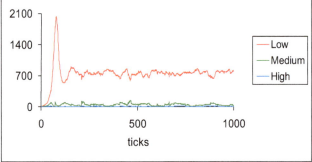

Figure 184: The evolution of number of turtles from low, medium and high class (`Low`, `Medium`, `High`) in the case of computer experiment `E4` `run 1`

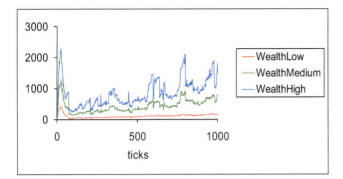

Figure 185: The evolution of global wealth of turtles from low, medium and high class (WealthLow, WealthMedium, WealthHigh) in the case of computer experiment E4 run 1

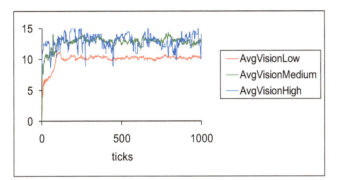

Figure 186: The evolution of turtles vision from low, medium and high class (AvgVisionLow, AvgVisionMedium, AvgVisionHigh) in the case of E4 computer experiment run 1

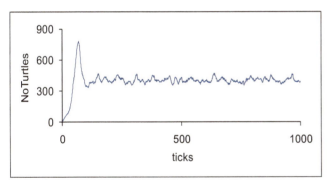

Figure 187: The evolution of turtles' population (NoTurtles) in the case of computer experiment E4 run 2

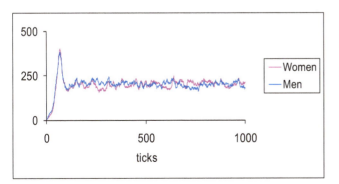

Figure 188: The evolution of female and male turtles (Women, and Men variables) in the case of computer experiment E4 run 2

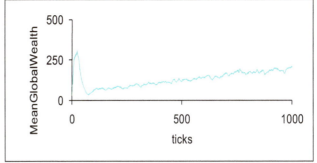

Figure 189: The evolution of average global wealth MeanGlobalWealth in the case of computer experiment E4 run 2

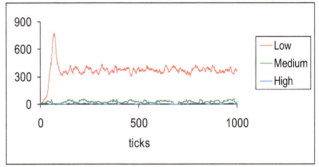

Figure 190: The evolution of number of turtles from low, medium and high class (Low, Medium, High) in the case of computer experiment E4 run 2

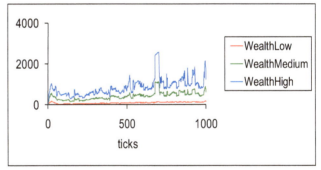

Figure 191: The evolution of global wealth of turtles from low, medium and high class (WealthLow, WealthMedium, WealthHigh) in the case of computer experiment E4 run 2

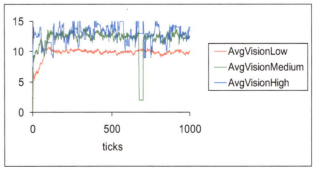

Figure 192: The evolution of turtles vision from low, medium and high class (AvgVisionLow, AvgVisionMedium, AvgVisionHigh) in the case of E4 computer experiment run 2

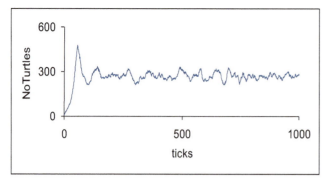

Figure 193: The evolution of turtles' population (NoTurtles) in the case of computer experiment E4 run 3

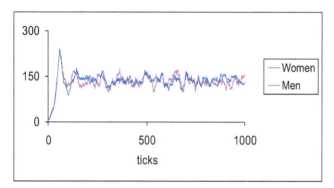

Figure 194: The evolution of female and male turtles (Women, and Men variables) in the case of computer experiment E4 run 3

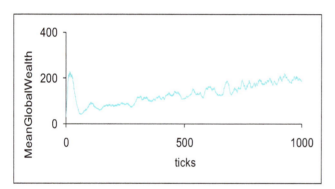

Figure 195: The evolution of average global wealth MeanGlobalWealth in the case of computer experiment E4 run 3

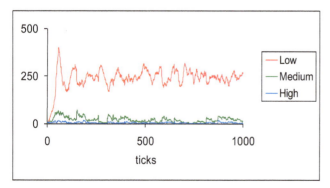

Figure 196: The evolution of number of turtles from low, medium and high class (Low, Medium, High) in the case of computer experiment E4 run 3

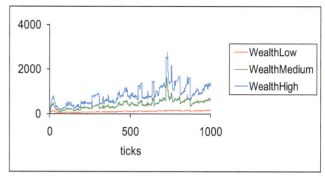

Figure 197: The evolution of global wealth of turtles from low, medium and high class (WealthLow, WealthMedium, WealthHigh) in the case of computer experiment E4 run 3

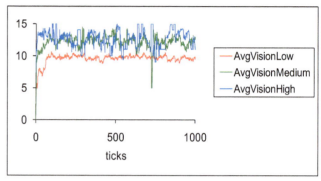

Figure 198: The evolution of turtles vision from low, medium and high class (AvgVisionLow, AvgVisionMedium, AvgVisionHigh) in the case of E4 computer experiment run 3

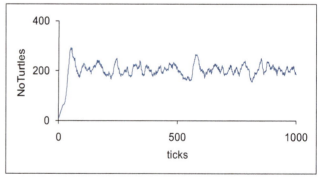

Figure 199: The evolution of turtles' population (NoTurtles) in the case of computer experiment E4 run 4

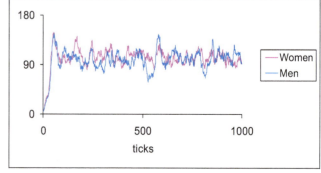

Figure 200: The evolution of female and male turtles (Women, and Men variables) in the case of computer experiment E4 run 4

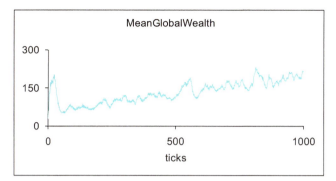

Figure 201: The evolution of average global wealth `MeanGlobalWealth` in the case of computer experiment `E4 run 4`

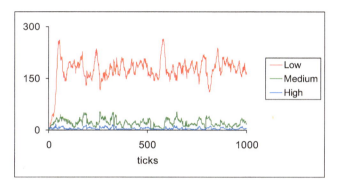

Figure 202: The evolution of number of turtles from low, medium and high class (`Low`, `Medium`, `High`) in the case of computer experiment `E4 run 4`

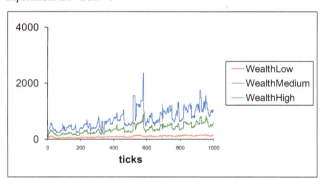

Figure 203: The evolution of global wealth of turtles from low, medium and high class (`WealthLow`, `WealthMedium`, `WealthHigh`) in the case of computer experiment `E4 run 4`

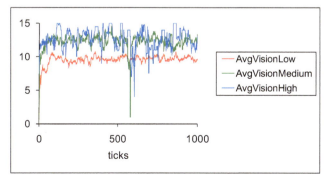

Figure 204: The evolution of turtles vision from low, medium and high class (`AvgVisionLow`, `AvgVisionMedium`, `AvgVisionHigh`) in the case of `E4` computer experiment `run 4`

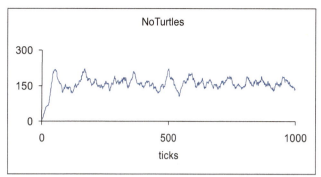

Figure 205: The evolution of turtles' population (`NoTurtles`) in the case of computer experiment `E4 run 5`

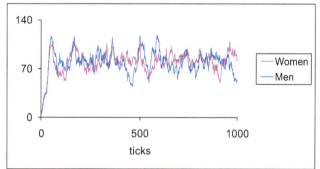

Figure 206: The evolution of female and male turtles (`Women`, and `Men` variables) in the case of computer experiment `E4 run 5`

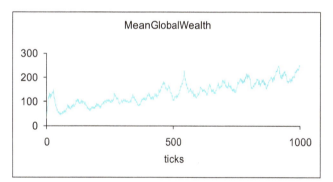

Figure 207: The evolution of average global wealth `MeanGlobalWealth` in the case of computer experiment `E4 run 5`

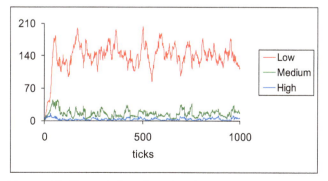

Figure 208: The evolution of number of turtles from low, medium and high class (`Low`, `Medium`, `High`) in the case of computer experiment `E4 run 5`

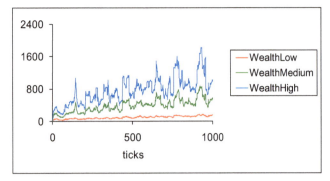

Figure 209: The evolution of global wealth of turtles from low, medium and high class (`WealthLow`, `WealthMedium`, `WealthHigh`) in the case of computer experiment `E4 run 5`

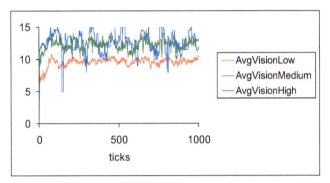

Figure 210: The evolution of turtles vision from low, medium and high class (`AvgVisionLow`, `AvgVisionMedium`, `AvgVisionHigh`) in the case of `E4` computer experiment `run 5`

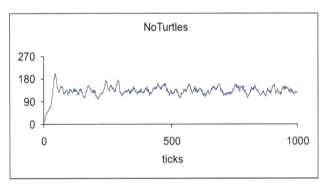

Figure 211: The evolution of turtles' population (`NoTurtles`) in the case of computer experiment `E3 run 6`

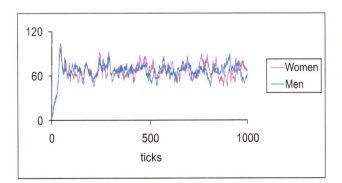

Figure 212: The evolution of female and male turtles (`Women`, and `Men` variables) in the case of computer experiment `E4 run 6`

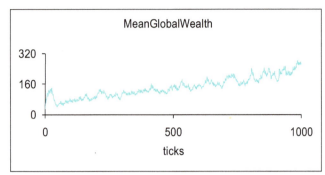

Figure 213: The evolution of average global wealth `MeanGlobalWealth` in the case of computer experiment `E4 run 6`

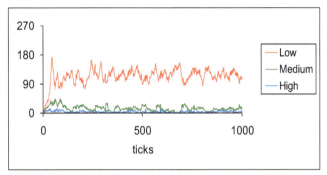

Figure 214: The evolution of number of turtles from low, medium and high class (`Low`, `Medium`, `High`) in the case of computer experiment `E4 run 6`

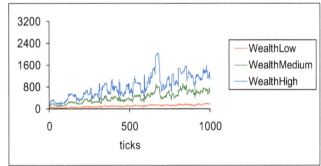

Figure 215: The evolution of global wealth of turtles from low, medium and high class (`WealthLow`, `WealthMedium`, `WealthHigh`) in the case of computer experiment `E4 run 6`

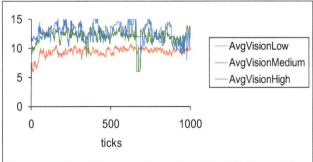

Figure 216: The evolution of turtles vision from low, medium and high class (`AvgVisionLow`, `AvgVisionMedium`, `AvgVisionHigh`) in the case of `E4` computer experiment `run 6`

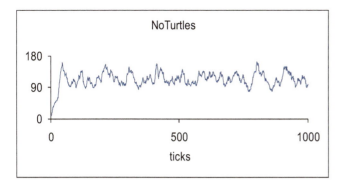

Figure 217: The evolution of turtles' population (`NoTurtles`) in the case of computer experiment `E4 run 7`

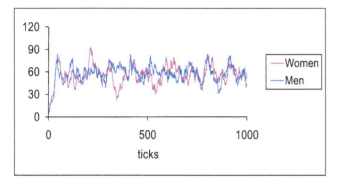

Figure 218: The evolution of female and male turtles (`Women`, and `Men` variables) in the case of computer experiment `E4 run 7`

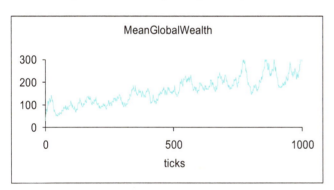

Figure 219: The evolution of average global wealth `MeanGlobalWealth` in the case of computer experiment `E4 run 7`

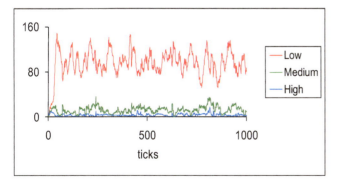

Figure 220: The evolution of number of turtles from low, medium and high class (`Low`, `Medium`, `High`) in the case of computer experiment `E4 run 7`

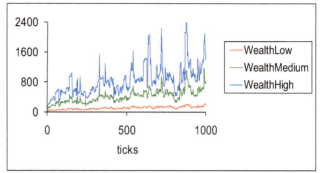

Figure 221: The evolution of global wealth of turtles from low, medium and high class (`WealthLow`, `WealthMedium`, `WealthHigh`) in the case of computer experiment `E4 run 7`

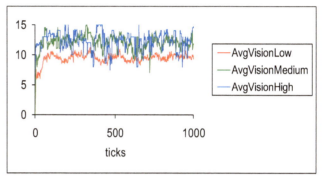

Figure 222: The evolution of turtles vision from low, medium and high class (`AvgVisionLow`, `AvgVisionMedium`, `AvgVisionHigh`) in the case of `E4` computer experiment `run 7`

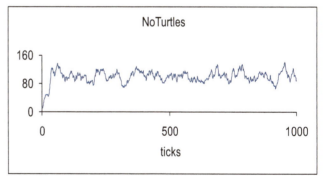

Figure 223: The evolution of turtles' population (`NoTurtles`) in the case of computer experiment `E4 run 8`

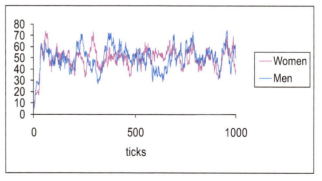

Figure 224: The evolution of female and male turtles (`Women`, and `Men` variables) in the case of computer experiment `E4 run 8`

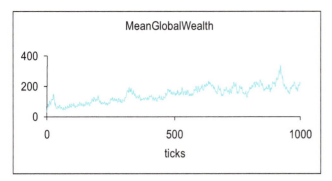

Figure 225: The evolution of average global wealth `MeanGlobalWealth` in the case of computer experiment `E4 run 9`

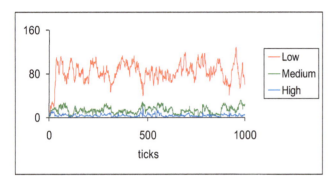

Figure 226: The evolution of number of turtles from low, medium and high class (`Low`, `Medium`, `High`) in the case of computer experiment `E4 run 8`

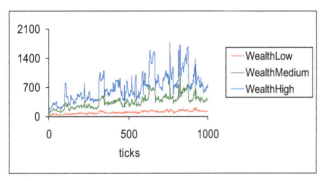

Figure 227: The evolution of global wealth of turtles from low, medium and high class (`WealthLow`, `WealthMedium`, `WealthHigh`) in the case of computer experiment `E4 run 8`

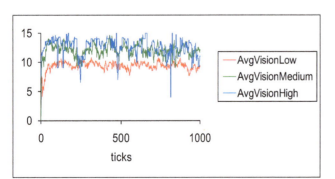

Figure 228: The evolution of turtles vision from low, medium and high class (`AvgVisionLow`, `AvgVisionMedium`, `AvgVisionHigh`) in the case of `E4` computer experiment `run 8`

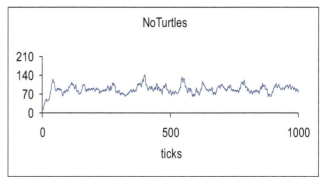

Figure 229: The evolution of turtles' population (`NoTurtles`) in the case of computer experiment `E4 run 9`

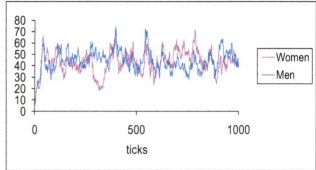

Figure 230: The evolution of female and male turtles (`Women`, and `Men` variables) in the case of computer experiment `E4 run 9`

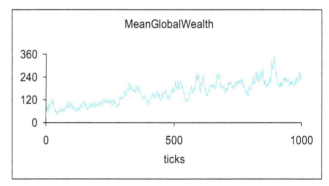

Figure 231: The evolution of average global wealth `MeanGlobalWealth` in the case of computer experiment `E4 run 9`

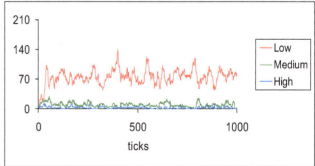

Figure 232: The evolution of number of turtles from low, medium and high class (`Low`, `Medium`, `High`) in the case of computer experiment `E4 run 9`

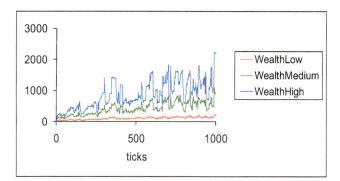

Figure 233: The evolution of global wealth of turtles from low, medium and high class (WealthLow, WealthMedium, WealthHigh) in the case of computer experiment E4 run 9

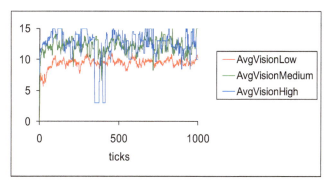

Figure 234: The evolution of turtles vision from low, medium and high class (AvgVisionLow, AvgVisionMedium, AvgVisionHigh) in the case of E4 computer experiment run 9

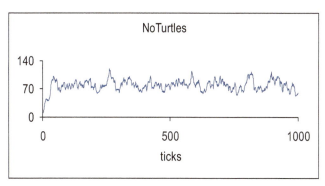

Figure 235: The evolution of turtles' population (NoTurtles) in the case of computer experiment E4 run 10

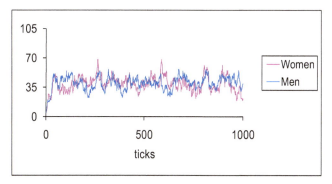

Figure 236: The evolution of female and male turtles (Women, and Men variables) in the case of computer experiment E4 run 10

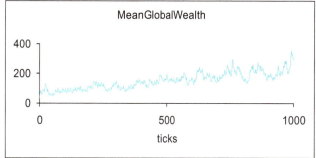

Figure 237: The evolution of average global wealth MeanGlobalWealth in the case of computer experiment E4 run 10

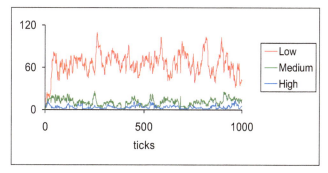

Figure 238: The evolution of number of turtles from low, medium and high class (Low, Medium, High) in the case of computer experiment E4 run 10

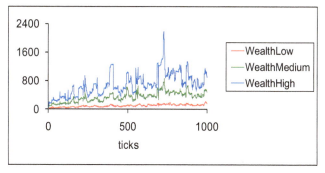

Figure 239: The evolution of global wealth of turtles from low, medium and high class (WealthLow, WealthMedium, WealthHigh) in the case of computer experiment E4 run 10

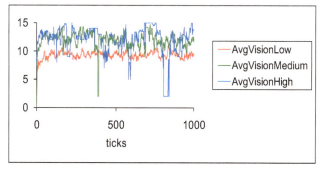

Figure 240: The evolution of turtles vision from low, medium and high class (AvgVisionLow, AvgVisionMedium, AvgVisionHigh) in the case of E4 computer experiment run 10

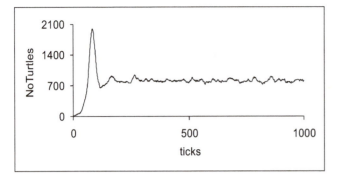

Figure 241: The evolution of turtles' population (NoTurtles) in the case of computer experiment E5 run 1

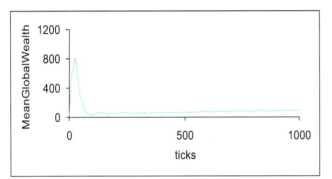

Figure 242: The evolution of female and male turtles (Women, and Men variables) in the case of computer experiment E5 run 1

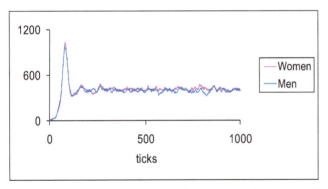

Figure 243: The evolution of average global wealth MeanGlobalWealth in the case of computer experiment E5 run 1

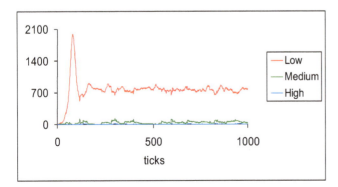

Figure 244: The evolution of number of turtles from low, medium and high class (Low, Medium, High) in the case of computer experiment E5 run 1

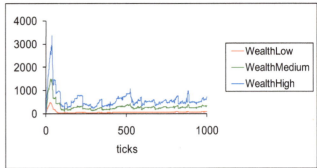

Figure 245: The evolution of global wealth of turtles from low, medium and high class (WealthLow, WealthMedium, WealthHigh) in the case of computer experiment E5 run 1

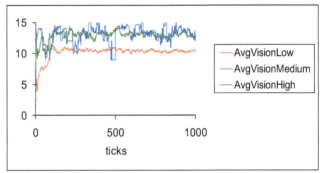

Figure 246: The evolution of turtles vision from low, medium and high class (AvgVisionLow, AvgVisionMedium, AvgVisionHigh) in the case of E5 computer experiment run 1

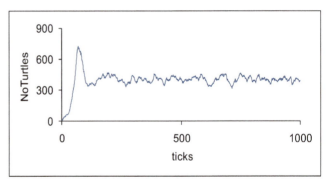

Figure 247: The evolution of turtles' population (NoTurtles) in the case of computer experiment E5 run 2

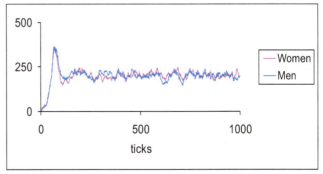

Figure 248: The evolution of female and male turtles (Women, and Men variables) in the case of computer experiment E5 run 2

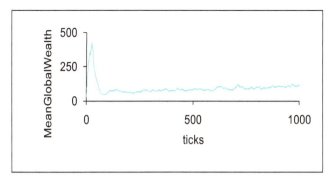

Figure 249: The evolution of average global wealth `MeanGlobalWealth` in the case of computer experiment E5 run 2

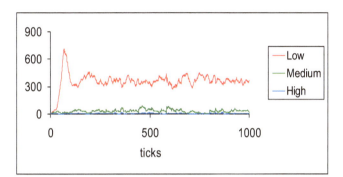

Figure 250: The evolution of number of turtles from low, medium and high class (`Low`, `Medium`, `High`) in the case of computer experiment E5 run 2

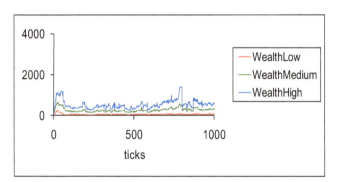

Figure 251: The evolution of global wealth of turtles from low, medium and high class (`WealthLow`, `WealthMedium`, `WealthHigh`) in the case of computer experiment E5 run 2

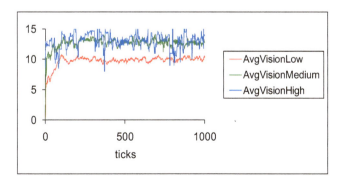

Figure 252: The evolution of turtles vision from low, medium and high class (`AvgVisionLow`, `AvgVisionMedium`, `AvgVisionHigh`) in the case of E5 computer experiment run 2

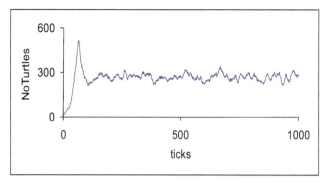

Figure 253: The evolution of turtles' population (`NoTurtles`) in the case of computer experiment E5 run 3

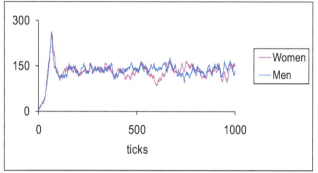

Figure 254: The evolution of female and male turtles (`Women`, and `Men` variables) in the case of computer experiment E5 run 3

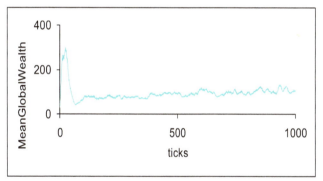

Figure 255: The evolution of average global wealth `MeanGlobalWealth` in the case of computer experiment E5 run 3

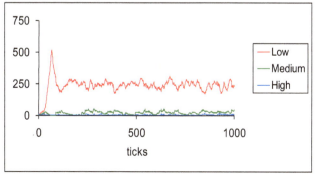

Figure 256: The evolution of number of turtles from low, medium and high class (`Low`, `Medium`, `High`) in the case of computer experiment E5 run 3

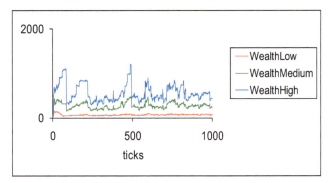

Figure 257: The evolution of global wealth of turtles from low, medium and high class (WealthLow, WealthMedium, WealthHigh) in the case of computer experiment E5 run 3

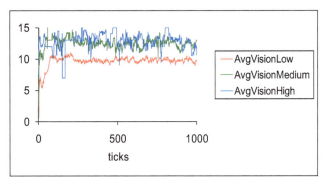

Figure 258: The evolution of turtles vision from low, medium and high class (AvgVisionLow, AvgVisionMedium, AvgVisionHigh) in the case of E5 computer experiment run 3

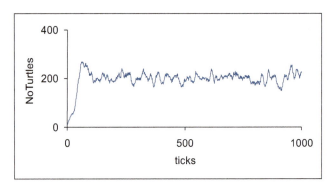

Figure 259: The evolution of turtles' population (NoTurtles) in the case of computer experiment E5 run 4

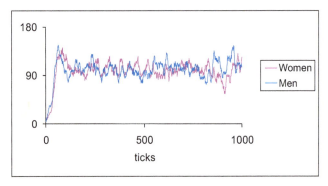

Figure 260: The evolution of female and male turtles (Women, and Men variables) in the case of computer experiment E5 run 4

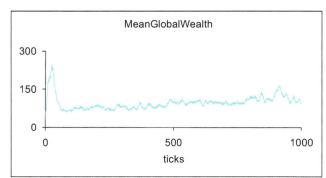

Figure 261: The evolution of average global wealth MeanGlobalWealth in the case of computer experiment E5 run 4

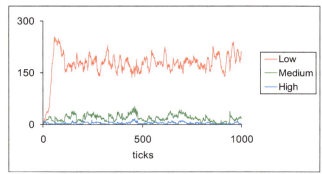

Figure 262: The evolution of number of turtles from low, medium and high class (Low, Medium, High) in the case of computer experiment E5 run 4

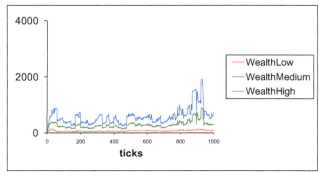

Figure 263: The evolution of global wealth of turtles from low, medium and high class (WealthLow, WealthMedium, WealthHigh) in the case of computer experiment E5 run 4

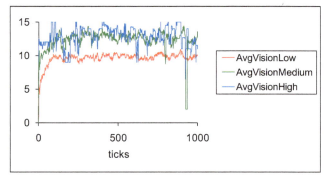

Figure 264: The evolution of turtles vision from low, medium and high class (AvgVisionLow, AvgVisionMedium, AvgVisionHigh) in the case of E5 computer experiment run 4

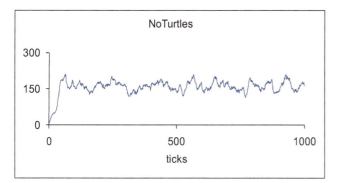

Figure 265: The evolution of turtles' population (`NoTurtles`) in the case of computer experiment `E5 run 5`

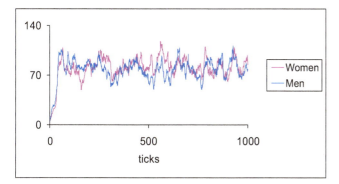

Figure 266: The evolution of female and male turtles (`Women`, and `Men` variables) in the case of computer experiment `E5 run 5`

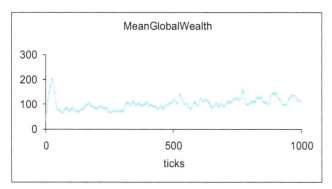

Figure 267: The evolution of average global wealth `MeanGlobalWealth` in the case of computer experiment `E5 run 5`

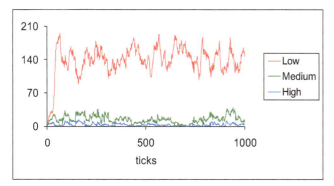

Figure 268: The evolution of number of turtles from low, medium and high class (`Low`, `Medium`, `High`) in the case of computer experiment `E5 run 5`

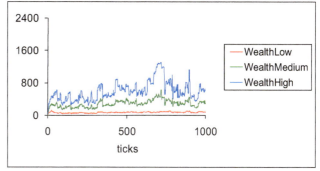

Figure 269: The evolution of global wealth of turtles from low, medium and high class (`WealthLow`, `WealthMedium`, `WealthHigh`) in the case of computer experiment `E5 run 5`

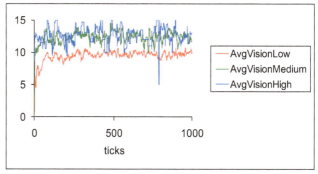

Figure 270: The evolution of turtles vision from low, medium and high class (`AvgVisionLow`, `AvgVisionMedium`, `AvgVisionHigh`) in the case of `E5` computer experiment `run 5`

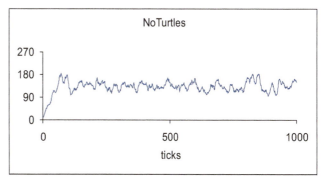

Figure 271: The evolution of turtles' population (`NoTurtles`) in the case of computer experiment `E5 run 6`

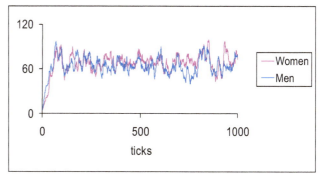

Figure 272: The evolution of female and male turtles (`Women`, and `Men` variables) in the case of computer experiment `E5 run 6`

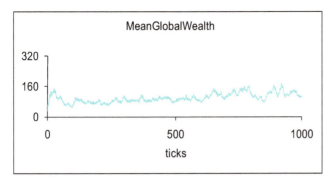

Figure 273: The evolution of average global wealth `MeanGlobalWealth` in the case of computer experiment E5 `run 6`

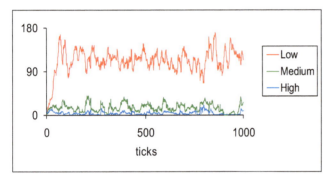

Figure 274: The evolution of number of turtles from low, medium and high class (`Low, Medium, High`) in the case of computer experiment E5 `run 6`

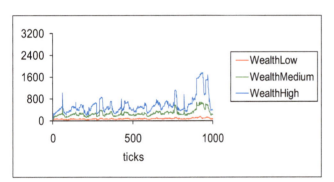

Figure 275: The evolution of global wealth of turtles from low, medium and high class (`WealthLow, WealthMedium, WealthHigh`) in the case of computer experiment E5 `run 6`

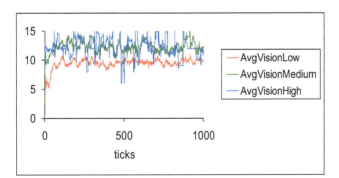

Figure 276: The evolution of turtles vision from low, medium and high class (`AvgVisionLow, AvgVisionMedium, AvgVisionHigh`) in the case of E5 computer experiment `run 6`

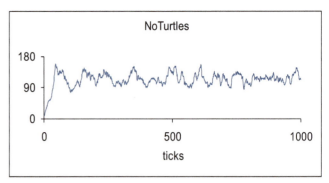

Figure 277: The evolution of turtles' population (`NoTurtles`) in the case of computer experiment E5 `run 7`

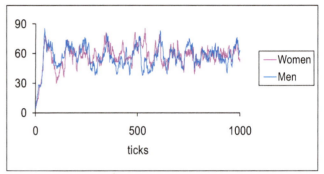

Figure 278: The evolution of female and male turtles (`Women`, and `Men` variables) in the case of computer experiment E5 `run 7`

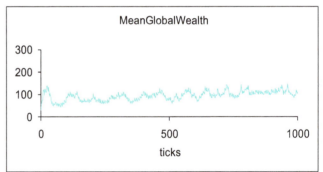

Figure 279: The evolution of average global wealth `MeanGlobalWealth` in the case of computer experiment E5 `run 7`

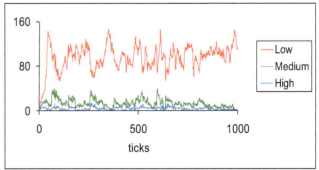

Figure 280: The evolution of number of turtles from low, medium and high class (`Low, Medium, High`) in the case of computer experiment E5 `run 7`

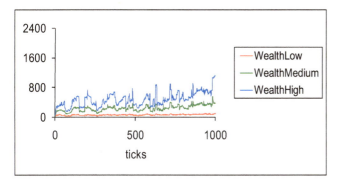

Figure 281: The evolution of global wealth of turtles from low, medium and high class (WealthLow, WealthMedium, WealthHigh) in the case of computer experiment E5 run 7

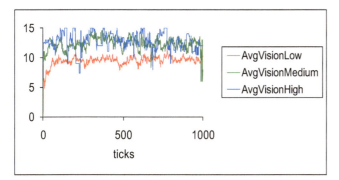

Figure 282: The evolution of turtles vision from low, medium and high class (AvgVisionLow, AvgVisionMedium, AvgVisionHigh) in the case of E5 computer experiment run 7

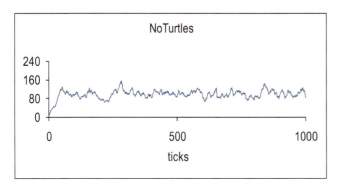

Figure 283: The evolution of turtles' population (NoTurtles) in the case of computer experiment E5 run 8

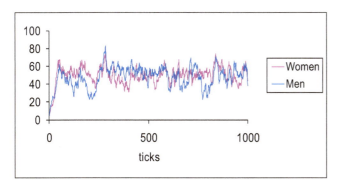

Figure 284: The evolution of female and male turtles (Women, and Men variables) in the case of computer experiment E5 run 8

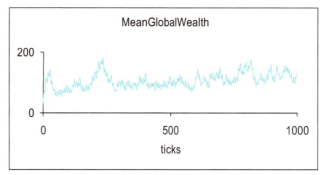

Figure 285: The evolution of average global wealth MeanGlobalWealth in the case of computer experiment E5 run 8

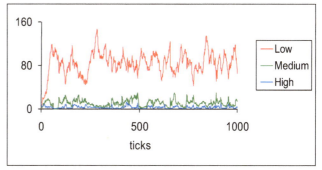

Figure 286: The evolution of number of turtles from low, medium and high class (Low, Medium, High) in the case of computer experiment E5 run 8

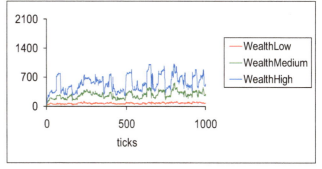

Figure 287: The evolution of global wealth of turtles from low, medium and high class (WealthLow, WealthMedium, WealthHigh) in the case of computer experiment E5 run 8

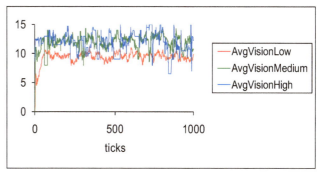

Figure 288: The evolution of turtles vision from low, medium and high class (AvgVisionLow, AvgVisionMedium, AvgVisionHigh) in the case of E5 computer experiment run 8

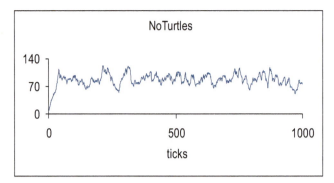

Figure 289: The evolution of turtles' population (NoTurtles) in the case of computer experiment E5 run 9

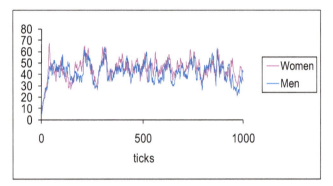

Figure 290: The evolution of female and male turtles (Women, and Men variables) in the case of computer experiment E5 run 9

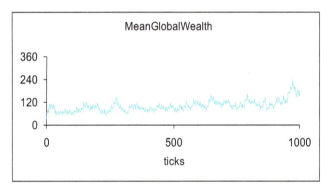

Figure 291: The evolution of average global wealth MeanGlobalWealth in the case of computer experiment E5 run 9

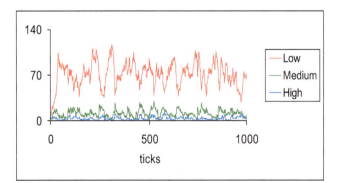

Figure 292: The evolution of number of turtles from low, medium and high class (Low, Medium, High) in the case of computer experiment E5 run 9

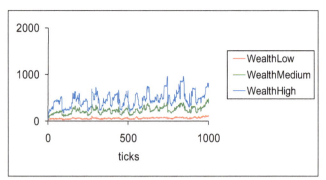

Figure 293: The evolution of global wealth of turtles from low, medium and high class (WealthLow, WealthMedium, WealthHigh) in the case of computer experiment E5 run 9

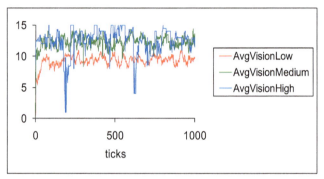

Figure 294: The evolution of turtles vision from low, medium and high class (AvgVisionLow, AvgVisionMedium, AvgVisionHigh) in the case of E5 computer experiment run 9

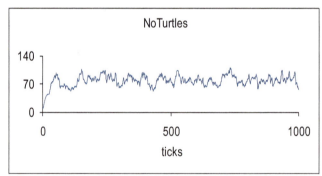

Figure 295: The evolution of turtles' population (NoTurtles) in the case of computer experiment E5 run 10

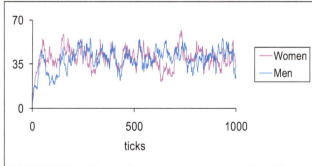

Figure 296: The evolution of female and male turtles (Women, and Men variables) in the case of computer experiment E5 run 10

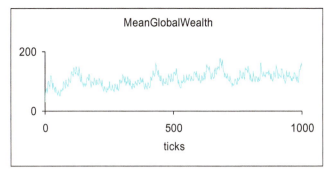

Figure 297: The evolution of average global wealth `MeanGlobalWealth` in the case of computer experiment `E5 run 10`

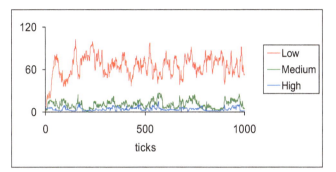

Figure 298: The evolution of number of turtles from low, medium and high class (`Low`, `Medium`, `High`) in the case of computer experiment `E5 run 10`

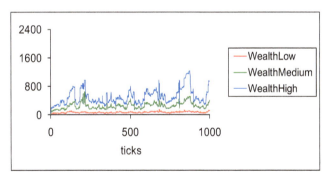

Figure 299: The evolution of global wealth of turtles from low, medium and high class (`WealthLow`, `WealthMedium`, `WealthHigh`) in the case of computer experiment `E5 run 10`

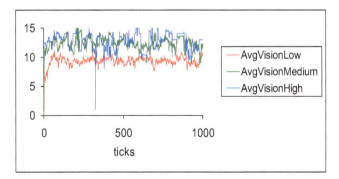

Figure 300: The evolution of turtles vision from low, medium and high class (`AvgVisionLow`, `AvgVisionMedium`, `AvgVisionHigh`) in the case of `E5` computer experiment `run 10`

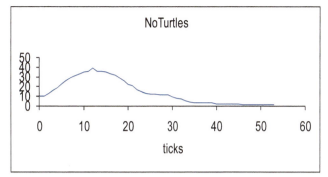

Figure 301: The evolution of turtles' population (`NoTurtles`) in the case of computer experiment `E6 run 1`

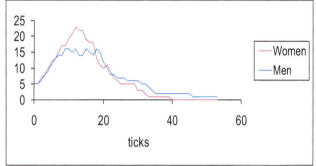

Figure 302: The evolution of female and male turtles (`Women`, and `Men` variables) in the case of computer experiment `E6 run 1`

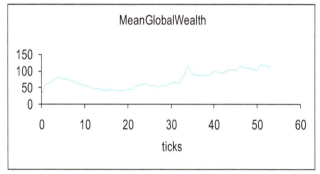

Figure 303: The evolution of average global wealth `MeanGlobalWealth` in the case of computer experiment `E6 run 1`

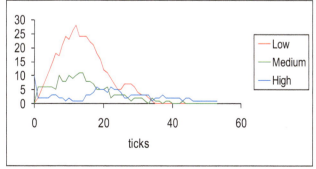

Figure 304: The evolution of number of turtles from low, medium and high class (`Low`, `Medium`, `High`) in the case of computer experiment `E6 run 1`

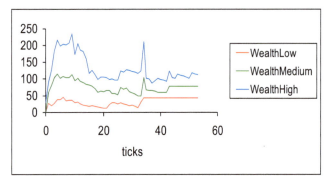

Figure 305: The evolution of global wealth of turtles from low, medium and high class (`WealthLow`, `WealthMedium`, `WealthHigh`) in the case of computer experiment `E6 run 1`

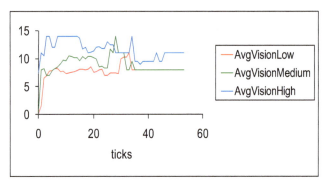

Figure 306: The evolution of turtles vision from low, medium and high class (`AvgVisionLow`, `AvgVisionMedium`, `AvgVisionHigh`) in the case of `E6` computer experiment `run 1`

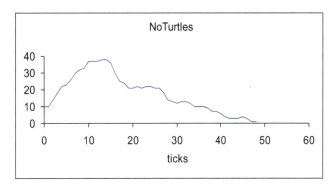

Figure 307: The evolution of turtles' population (`NoTurtles`) in the case of computer experiment `E6 run 2`

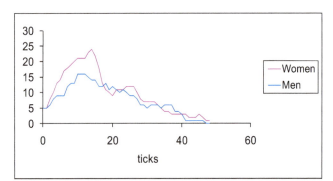

Figure 308: The evolution of female and male turtles (`Women`, and `Men` variables) in the case of computer experiment `E6 run 2`

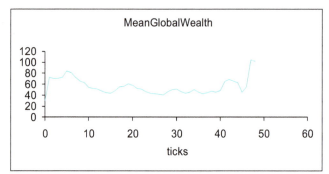

Figure 309: The evolution of average global wealth `MeanGlobalWealth` in the case of computer experiment `E6 run 2`

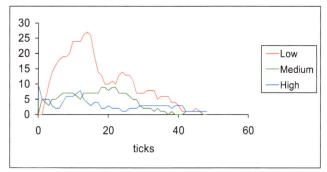

Figure 310: The evolution of number of turtles from low, medium and high class (`Low`, `Medium`, `High`) in the case of computer experiment `E6 run 2`

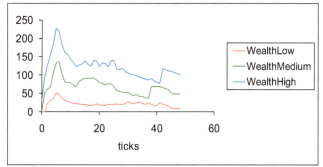

Figure 311: The evolution of global wealth of turtles from low, medium and high class (`WealthLow`, `WealthMedium`, `WealthHigh`) in the case of computer experiment `E6 run 2`

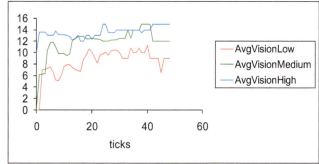

Figure 312: The evolution of turtles vision from low, medium and high class (`AvgVisionLow`, `AvgVisionMedium`, `AvgVisionHigh`) in the case of `E6` computer experiment `run 2`

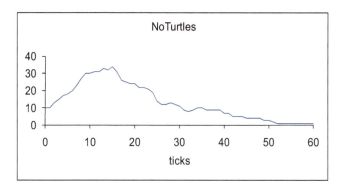

Figure 313: The evolution of turtles' population (`NoTurtles`) in the case of computer experiment `E6 run 3`

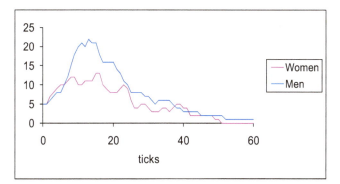

Figure 314: The evolution of female and male turtles (`Women`, and `Men` variables) in the case of computer experiment `E6 run 3`

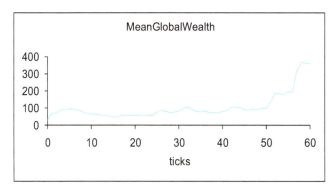

Figure 315: The evolution of average global wealth `MeanGlobalWealth` in the case of computer experiment `E6 run 3`

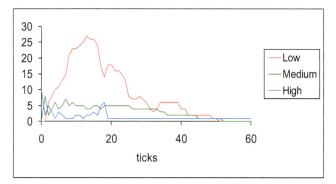

Figure 316: The evolution of number of turtles from low, medium and high class (`Low`, `Medium`, `High`) in the case of computer experiment `E6 run 3`

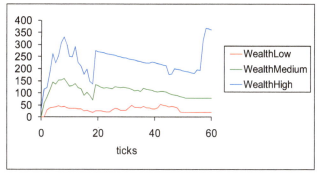

Figure 317: The evolution of global wealth of turtles from low, medium and high class (`WealthLow`, `WealthMedium`, `WealthHigh`) in the case of computer experiment `E6 run 3`

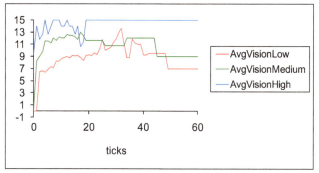

Figure 318: The evolution of turtles vision from low, medium and high class (`AvgVisionLow`, `AvgVisionMedium`, `AvgVisionHigh`) in the case of `E6` computer experiment `run 3`

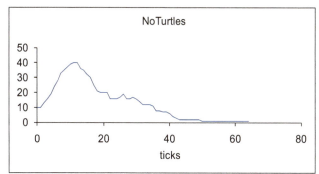

Figure 319: The evolution of turtles' population (`NoTurtles`) in the case of computer experiment `E6 run 4`

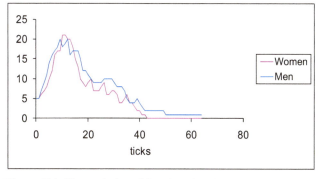

Figure 320: The evolution of female and male turtles (`Women`, and `Men` variables) in the case of computer experiment `E6 run 4`

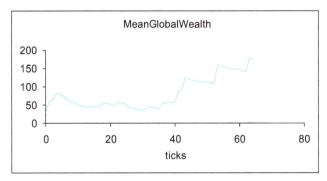

Figure 321: The evolution of average global wealth `MeanGlobalWealth` in the case of computer experiment `E6 run 4`

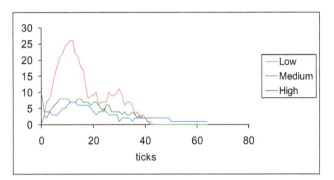

Figure 322: The evolution of number of turtles from low, medium and high class (`Low`, `Medium`, `High`) in the case of computer experiment `E6 run 4`

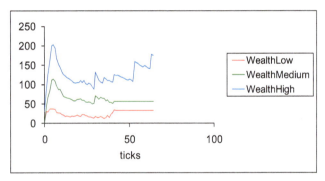

Figure 323: The evolution of global wealth of turtles from low, medium and high class (`WealthLow`, `WealthMedium`, `WealthHigh`) in the case of computer experiment `E6 run 4`

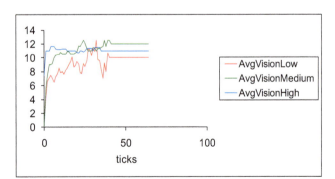

Figure 324: The evolution of turtles vision from low, medium and high class (`AvgVisionLow`, `AvgVisionMedium`, `AvgVisionHigh`) in the case of `E6` computer experiment `run 4`

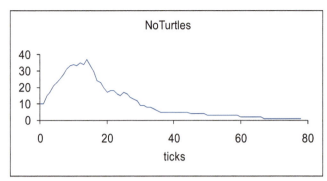

Figure 325: The evolution of turtles' population (`NoTurtles`) in the case of computer experiment `E6 run 5`

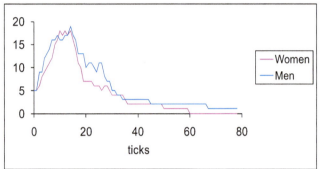

Figure 326: The evolution of female and male turtles (`Women`, and `Men` variables) in the case of computer experiment `E6 run 5`

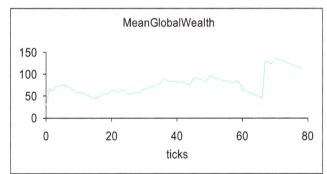

Figure 327: The evolution of average global wealth `MeanGlobalWealth` in the case of computer experiment `E6 run 5`

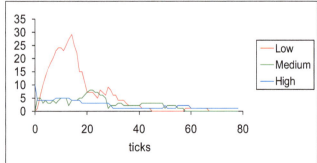

Figure 328: The evolution of number of turtles from low, medium and high class (`Low`, `Medium`, `High`) in the case of computer experiment `E6 run 5`

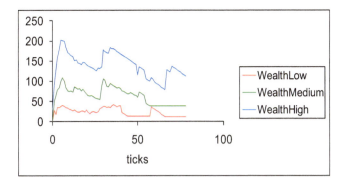 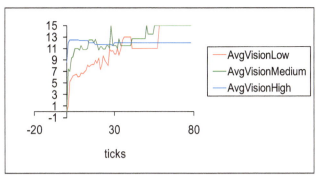

Figure 329: The evolution of global wealth of turtles from low, medium and high class (`WealthLow`, `WealthMedium`, `WealthHigh`) in the case of computer experiment `E6 run 5`

Figure 330: The evolution of turtles vision from low, medium and high class (`AvgVisionLow`, `AvgVisionMedium`, `AvgVisionHigh`) in the case of `E6` computer experiment `run 5`

APPENDIX 2

In this appendix, we describe the evolution of a new set of data that contain the average values for the variables `NoTurtles`, `Women`, `Men`, `MeanGlobalWealth`, `Low`, `Medium`, `High`, `AvgVisionLow`, `AvgVisionMedium`, `AvgVisionHigh`, `WealthLow`, `WealthMedium`, and `WealthHigh` for computer experiments E1-E5 when resources are renewable.

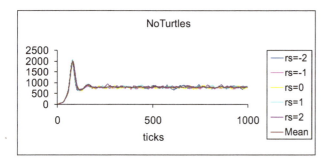

Figure 1: The evolution of `NoTurtles` in the case of `Interval = 1`

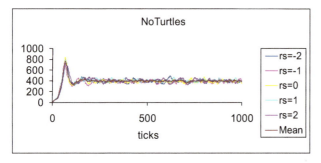

Figure 2: The evolution of `NoTurtles` in the case of `Interval = 2`

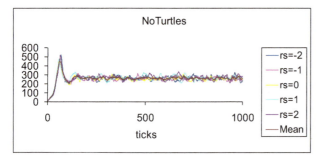

Figure 3: The evolution of `NoTurtles` in the case of `Interval = 3`

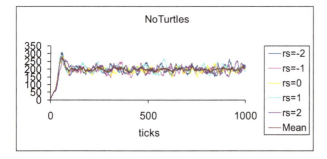

Figure 4: The evolution of `NoTurtles` in the case of `Interval = 4`

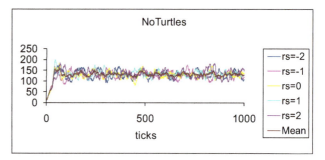

Figure 5: The evolution of `NoTurtles` in the case of `Interval = 5`

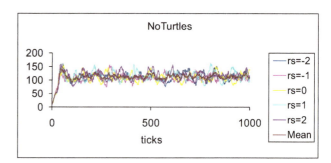

Figure 6: The evolution of `NoTurtles` in the case of `Interval = 6`

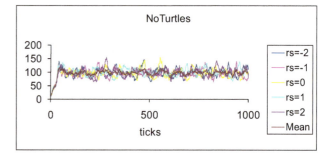

Figure 7: The evolution of `NoTurtles` in the case of `Interval = 7`

Figure 8: The evolution of `NoTurtles` in the case of `Interval = 8`

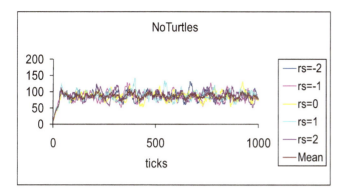

Figure 9: The evolution of `NoTurtles` in the case of `Interval = 9`

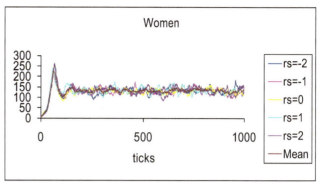

Figure 13: The evolution of `Women` in the case of `Interval = 3`

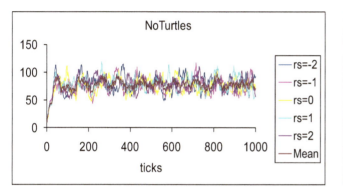

Figure 10: The evolution of `NoTurtles` in the case of `Interval = 10`

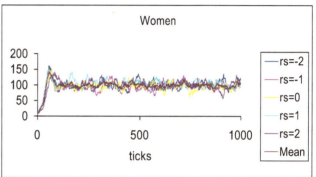

Figure 14: The evolution of `Women` in the case of `Interval = 4`

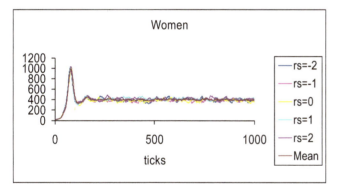

Figure 11: The evolution of `Women` in the case of `Interval = 1`

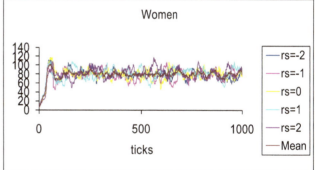

Figure 15: The evolution of `Women` in the case of `Interval = 5`

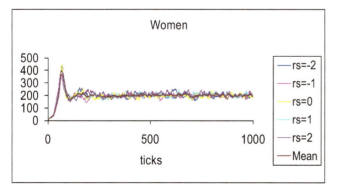

Figure 12: The evolution of `Women` in the case of `Interval = 2`

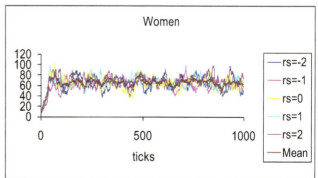

Figure 16: The evolution of `Women` in the case of `Interval = 6`

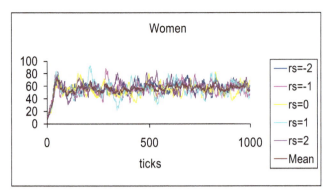

Figure 17: The evolution of Women in the case of Interval = 7

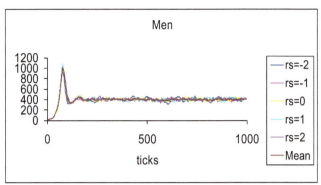

Figure 21: The evolution of Men in the case of Interval = 1

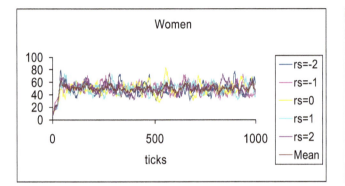

Figure 18: The evolution of Women in the case of Interval = 8

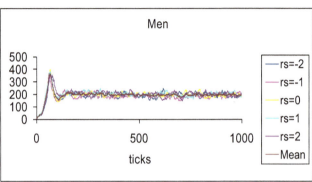

Figure 22: The evolution of Men in the case of Interval = 2

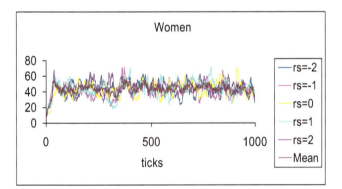

Figure 19: The evolution of Women in the case of Interval = 9

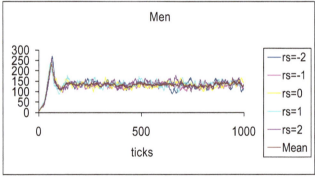

Figure 23: The evolution of Men in the case of Interval = 3

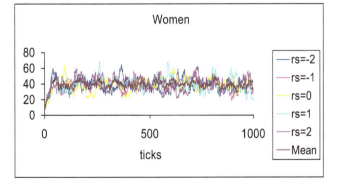

Figure 20: The evolution of Women in the case of Interval = 10

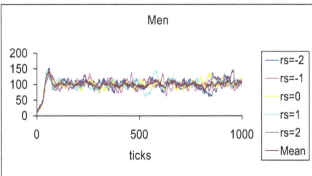

Figure 24: The evolution of Men in the case of Interval = 4

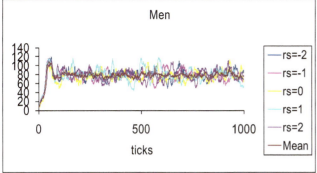

Figure 25: The evolution of Men in the case of Interval = 5

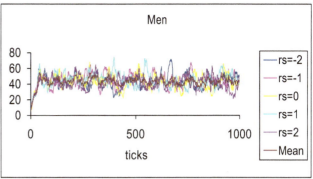

Figure 29: The evolution of Men in the case of Interval = 9

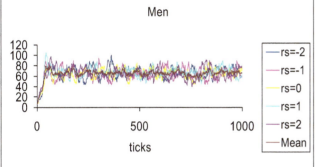

Figure 26: The evolution of Men in the case of Interval = 6

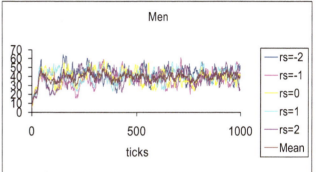

Figure 30: The evolution of Men in the case of Interval = 10

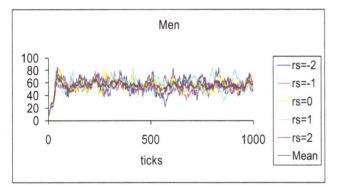

Figure 27: The evolution of Men in the case of Interval = 7

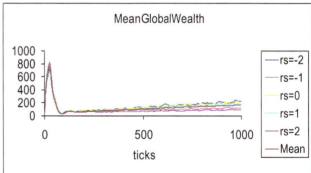

Figure 31: The evolution of MeanGlobalWealth in the case of Interval = 1

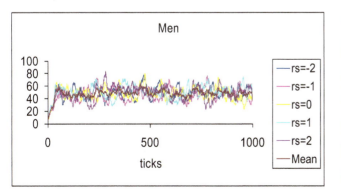

Figure 28: The evolution of Men in the case of Interval = 8

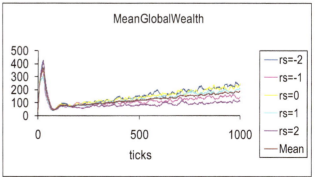

Figure 32: The evolution of MeanGlobalWealth in the case of Interval = 2

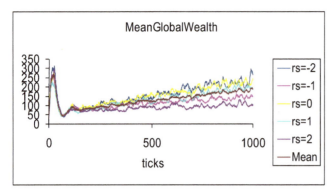

Figure 33: The evolution of `MeanGlobalWealth` in the case of `Interval = 3`

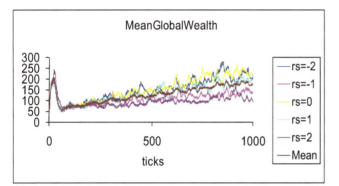

Figure 34: The evolution of `MeanGlobalWealth` in the case of `Interval = 4`

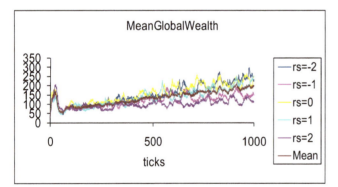

Figure 35: The evolution of `MeanGlobalWealth` in the case of `Interval = 5`

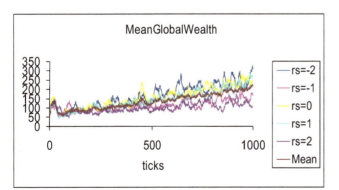

Figure 36: The evolution of `MeanGlobalWealth` in the case of `Interval = 6`

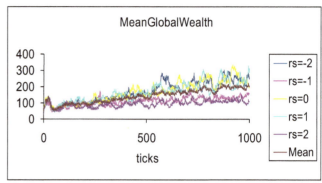

Figure 37: The evolution of `MeanGlobalWealth` in the case of `Interval = 7`

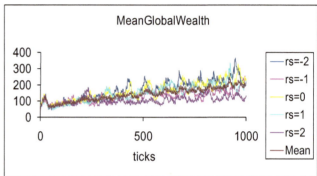

Figure 38: The evolution of `MeanGlobalWealth` in the case of `Interval = 8`

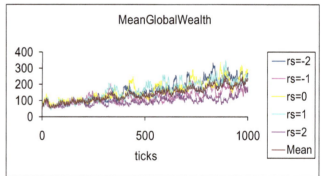

Figure 39: The evolution of `MeanGlobalWealth` in the case of `Interval = 9`

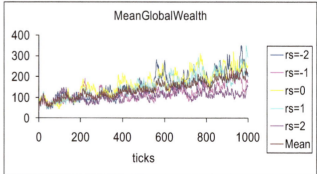

Figure 40: The evolution of `MeanGlobalWealth` in the case of `Interval = 10`

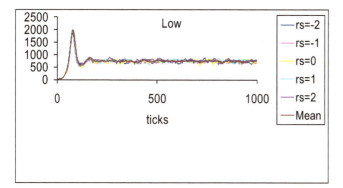

Figure 41: The evolution of Low in the case of Interval = 1

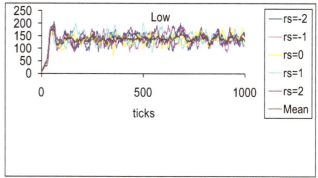

Figure 45: The evolution of Low in the case of Interval = 5

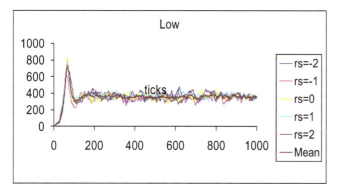

Figure 42: The evolution of Low in the case of Interval = 2

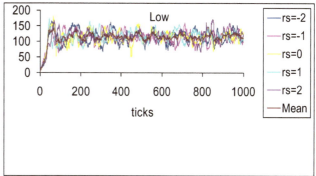

Figure 46: The evolution of Low in the case of Interval = 6

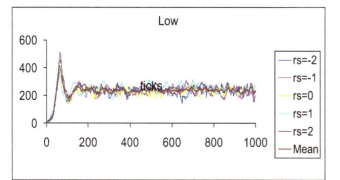

Figure 43: The evolution of Low in the case of Interval = 3

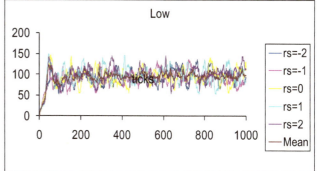

Figure 47: The evolution of Low in the case of Interval = 7

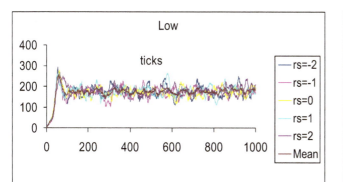

Figure 44: The evolution of Low in the case of Interval = 4

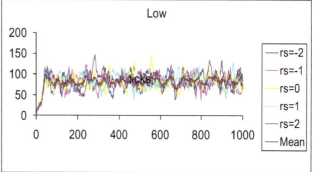

Figure 48: The evolution of Low in the case of Interval = 8

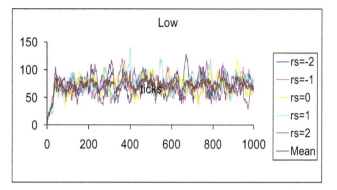

Figure 49: The evolution of `Low` in the case of `Interval` = 9

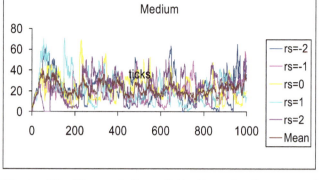

Figure 53: The evolution of `Medium` in the case of `Interval` = 3

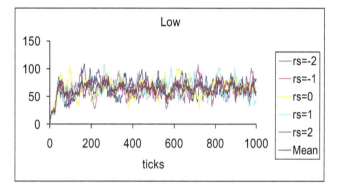

Figure 50: The evolution of `Low` in the case of `Interval` = 10

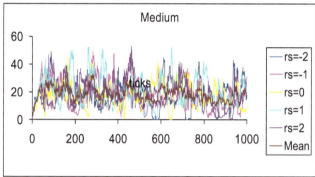

Figure 54: The evolution of `Medium` in the case of `Interval` = 4

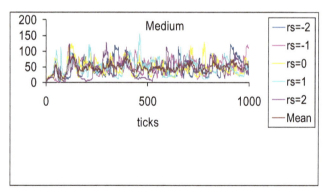

Figure 51: The evolution of `Medium` in the case of `Interval` = 1

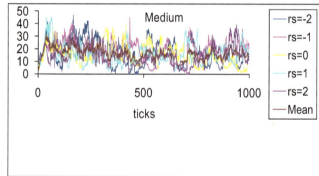

Figure 55: The evolution of `Medium` in the case of `Interval` = 5

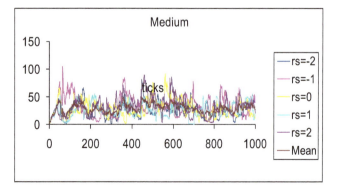

Figure 52: The evolution of `Medium` in the case of `Interval` = 2

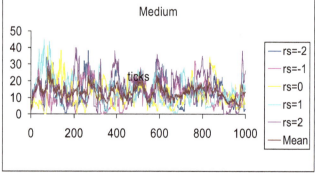

Figure 56: The evolution of `Medium` in the case of `Interval` = 6

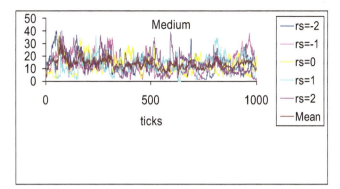

Figure 57: The evolution of Medium in the case of Interval = 7

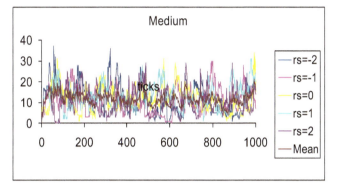

Figure 58: The evolution of Medium in the case of Interval = 8

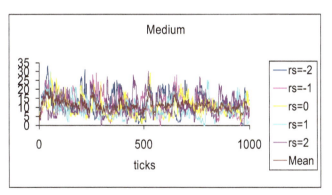

Figure 59: The evolution of Medium in the case of Interval = 9

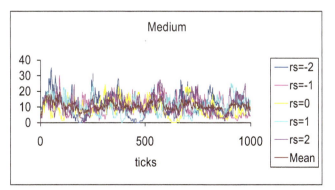

Figure 60: The evolution of Medium in the case of Apterval = 10

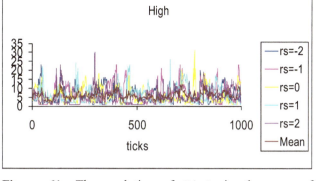

Figure 61: The evolution of High in the case of Interval = 1

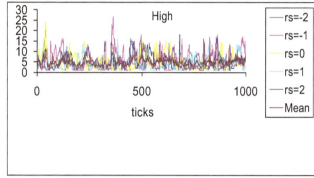

Figure 62: The evolution of High in the case of Interval = 2

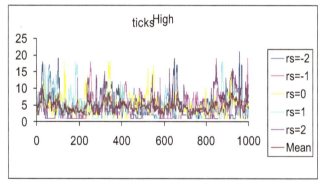

Figure 63: The evolution of High in the case of Interval = 3

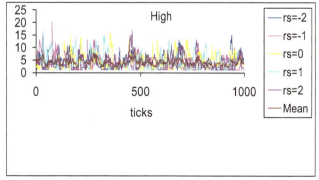

Figure 64: The evolution of High in the case of Interval = 4

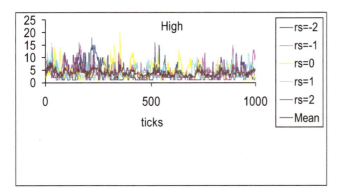

Figure 65: The evolution of High in the case of Interval = 5

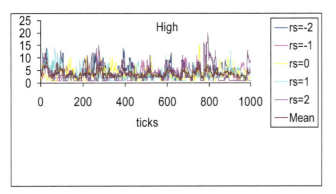

Figure 66: The evolution of High in the case of Interval = 6

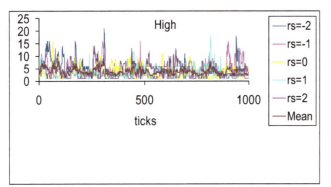

Figure 67: The evolution of High in the case of Interval = 7

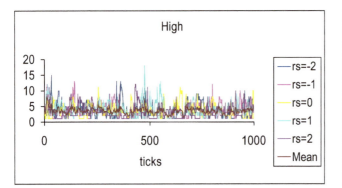

Figure 68: The evolution of High in the case of Interval = 8

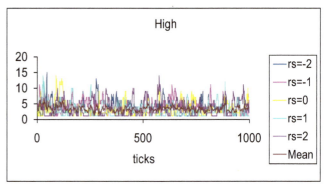

Figure 69: The evolution of High in the case of Interval = 9

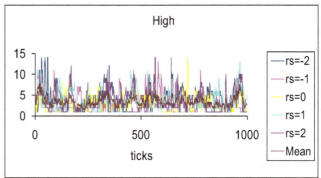

Figure 70: The evolution of High in the case of Interval = 10

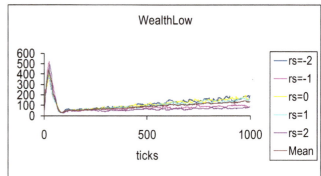

Figure 71: The evolution of WealthLow in the case of Interval = 1

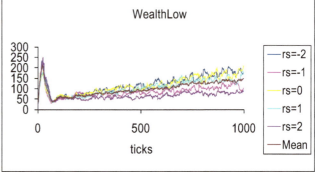

Figure 72: The evolution of WealthLow in the case of Interval = 2

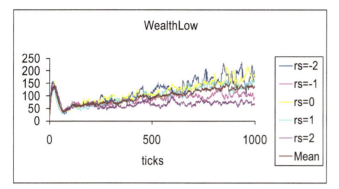

Figure 73: The evolution of `WealthLow` in the case of `Interval = 3`

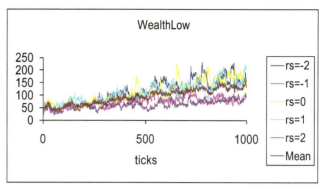

Figure 77: The evolution of `WealthLow` in the case of `Interval = 7`

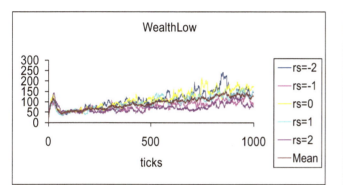

Figure 74: The evolution of `WealthLow` in the case of `Interval = 4`

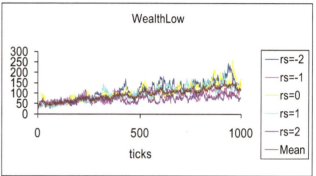

Figure 78: The evolution of `WealthLow` in the case of `Interval = 8`

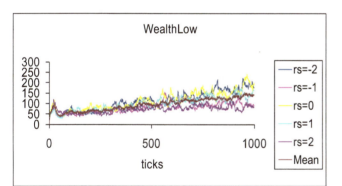

Figure 75: The evolution of `WealthLow` in the case of `Interval = 5`

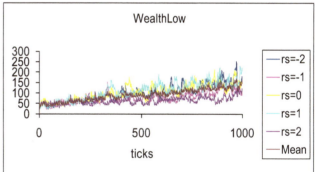

Figure 79: The evolution of `WealthLow` in the case of `Interval = 9`

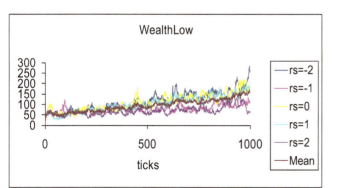

Figure 76: The evolution of `WealthLow` in the case of `Anterval = 6`

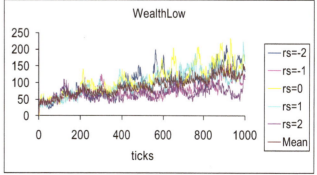

Figure 80: The evolution of `WealthLow` in the case of `Interval = 10`

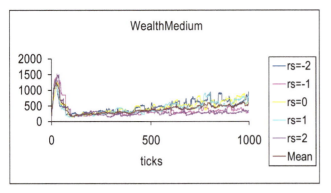

Figure 81: The evolution of WealthMedium in the case of Interval = 1

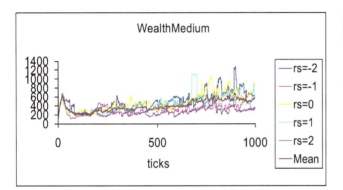

Figure 82: The evolution of WealthMedium in the case of Interval = 2

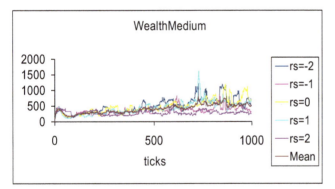

Figure 83: The evolution of WealthMedium in the case of Interval = 3

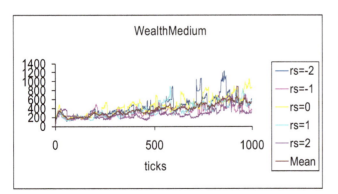

Figure 84: The evolution of WealthMedium in the case of Interval = 4

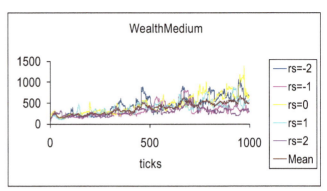

Figure 85: The evolution of WealthMedium in the case of Interval = 5

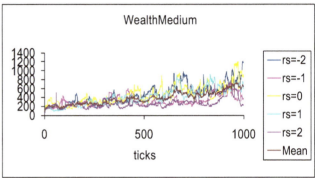

Figure 86: The evolution of WealthMedium in the case of Interval = 6

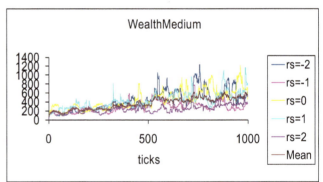

Figure 87: The evolution of WealthMedium in the case of Interval = 7

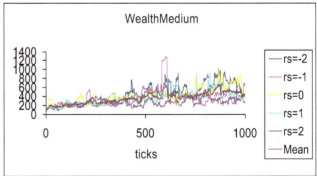

Figure 88: The evolution of WealthMedium in the case of Interval = 8

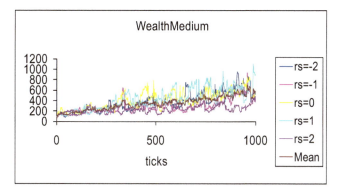

Figure 89: The evolution of `WealthMedium` in the case of `Interval = 9`

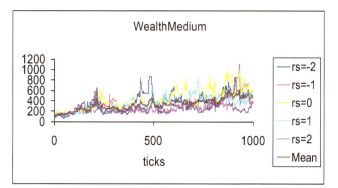

Figure 90: The evolution of `WealthMedium` in the case of `Interval = 10`

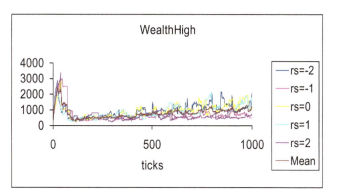

Figure 91: The evolution of `WealthHigh` in the case of `Interval = 1`

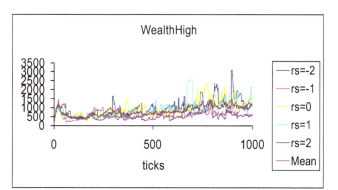

Figure 92: The evolution of `WealthHigh` in the case of `Interval = 2`

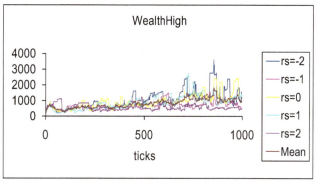

Figure 93: The evolution of `WealthHigh` in the case of `Interval = 3`

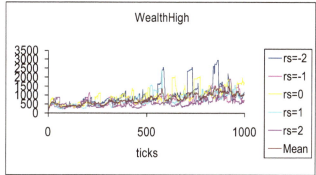

Figure 94: The evolution of `WealthHigh` in the case of `Interval = 4`

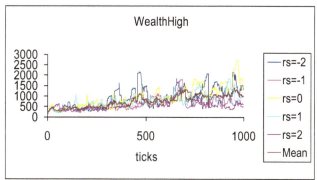

Figure 95: The evolution of `WealthHigh` in the case of `Interval = 5`

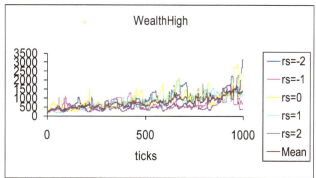

Figure 96: The evolution of `WealthHigh` in the case of `Interval = 6`

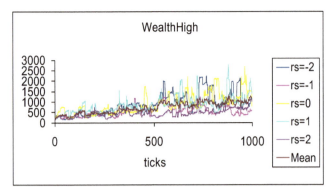

Figure 97: The evolution of `WealthHigh` in the case of `Interval = 7`

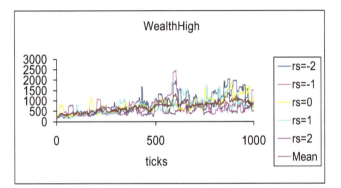

Figure 98: The evolution of `WealthHigh` in the case of `Interval = 8`

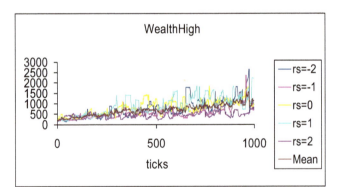

Figure 99: The evolution of `WealthHigh` in the case of `Interval = 9`

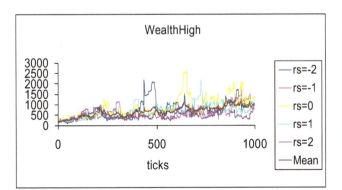

Figure 100: The evolution of `WealthHigh` in the case of `Interval = 10`

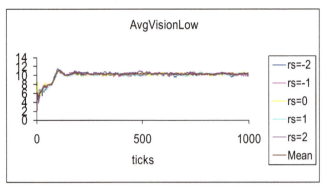

Figure 101: The evolution of `AvgVisionLow` in the case of `Interval = 1`

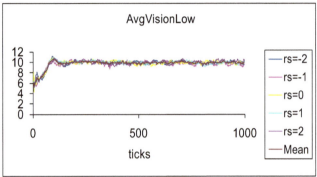

Figure 102: The evolution of `AvgVisionLow` in the case of `Interval = 2`

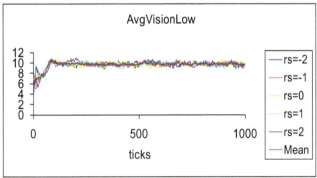

Figure 103: The evolution of `AvgVisionLow` in the case of `Interval = 3`

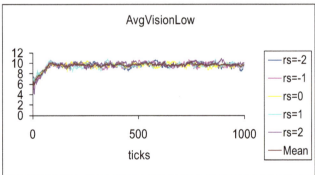

Figure 104: The evolution of `AvgVisionLow` in the case of `Interval = 4`

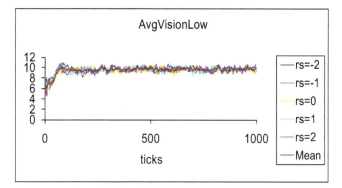

Figure 105: The evolution of `AvgVisionLow` in the case of `Interval = 5`

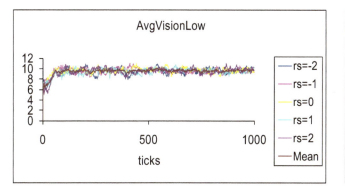

Figure 106: The evolution of `AvgVisionLow` in the case of `Interval = 6`

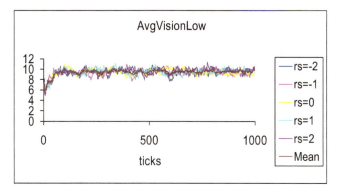

Figure 107: The evolution of `AvgVisionLow` in the case of `Interval = 7`

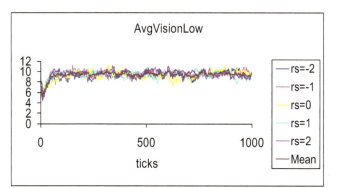

Figure 108: The evolution of `AvgVisionLow` in the case of `Interval = 8`

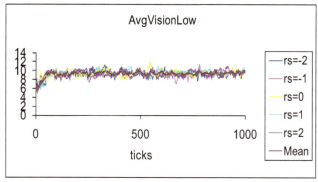

Figure 109: The evolution of `AvgVisionLow` in the case of `Interval = 9`

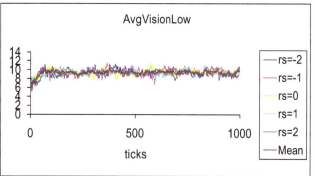

Figure 110: The evolution of `AvgVisionLow` in the case of `Interval = 10`

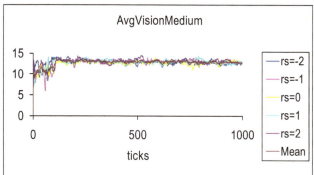

Figure 111: The evolution of `AvgVisionMedium` in the case of `Interval = 1`

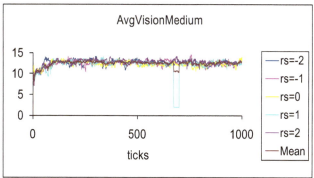

Figure 112: The evolution of `AvgVisionMedium` in the case of `Interval = 2`

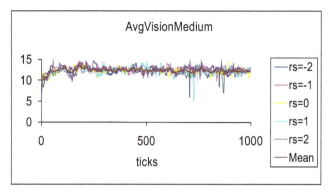

Figure 113: The evolution of AvgVisionMedium in the case of Interval = 3

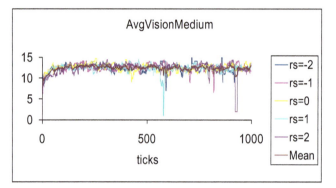

Figure 114: The evolution of AvgVisionMedium in the case of Interval = 4

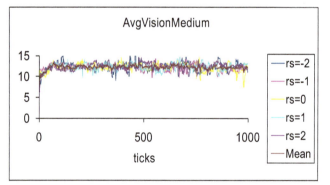

Figure 115: The evolution of AvgVisionMedium in the case of Interval = 5

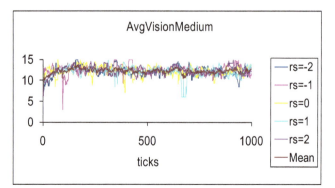

Figure 116: The evolution of AvgVisionMedium in the case of Interval = 6

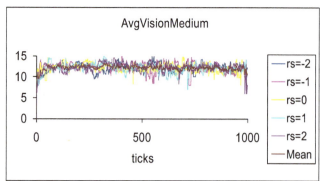

Figure 117: The evolution of AvgVisionMedium in the case of Interval = 7

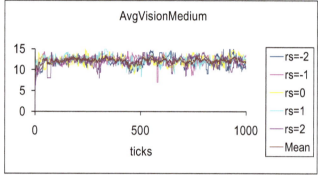

Figure 118: The evolution of AvgVisionMedium in the case of Interval = 8

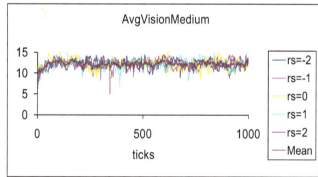

Figure 119: The evolution of AvgVisionMedium in the case of Interval = 9

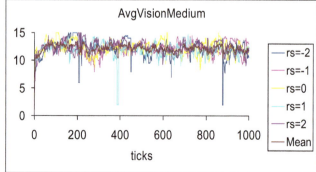

Figure 120: The evolution of AvgVisionMedium in the case of Interval = 10

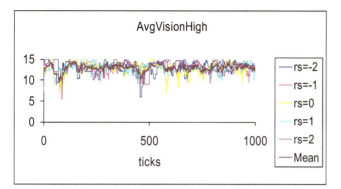

Figure 121: The evolution of `AvgVisionHigh` in the case of `Interval = 1`

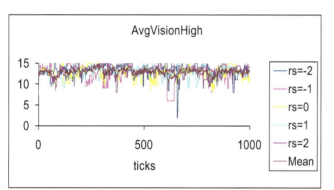

Figure 122: The evolution of `AvgVisionHigh` in the case of `Interval = 2`

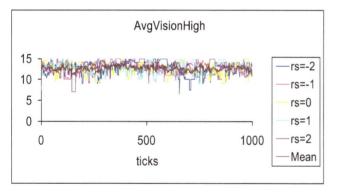

Figure 123: The evolution of `AvgVisionHigh` in the case of `Interval = 3`

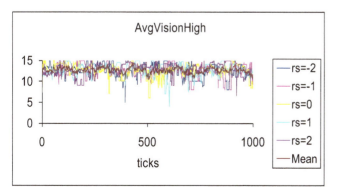

Figure 124: The evolution of `AvgVisionHigh` in the case of `Interval = 4`

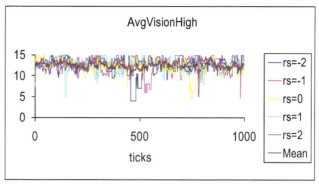

Figure 125: The evolution of `AvgVisionHigh` in the case of `Interval = 5`

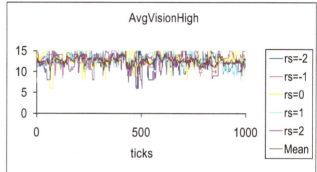

Figure 126: The evolution of `AvgVisionHigh` in the case of `Interval = 6`

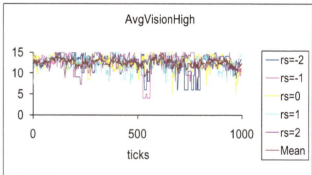

Figure 127: The evolution of `AvgVisionHigh` in the case of `Interval = 7`

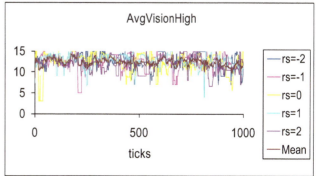

Figure 128: The evolution of `AvgVisionHigh` in the case of `Interval = 8`

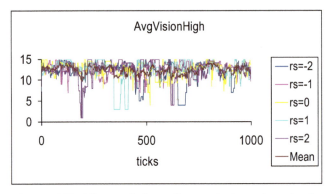

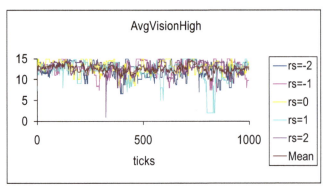

Figure 129: The evolution of `AvgVisionHigh` in the case of `Interval = 9`

Figure 130: The evolution of `avgvisionhigh` in the case of `interval = 10`

APPENDIX 3

In this appendix, we describe the evolution of a new set of data that contain the average values for the variables `NoTurtles`, `Women`, `Men`, `MeanGlobalWealth`, `Low`, `Medium`, `High`, `AvgVisionLow`, `AvgVisionMedium`, `AvgVisionHigh`, `WealthLow`, `WealthMedium`, and `WealthHigh` for computer experiment E6 when resources are nonrenewable.

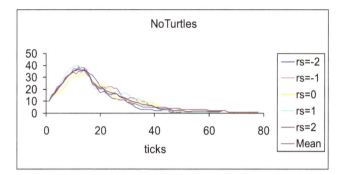

Figure 1: The evolution of `NoTurtles`

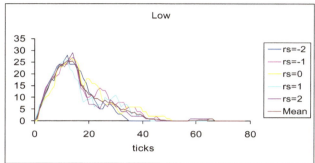

Figure 5: The evolution of `Low`

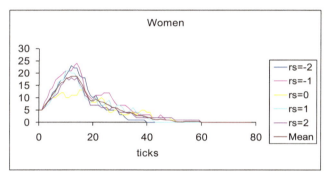

Figure 2: The evolution of `Women`

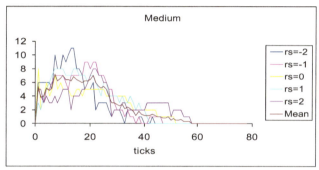

Figure 6: The evolution of `Medium`

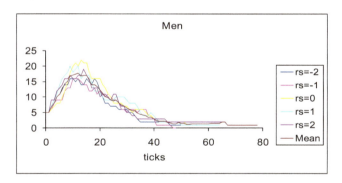

Figure 3: The evolution of `Men`

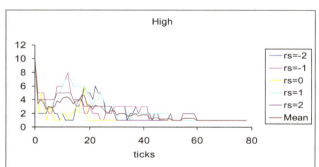

Figure 7: The evolution of `High`

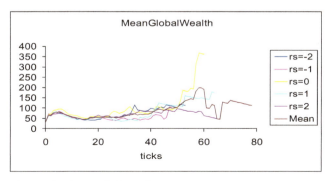

Figure 4: The evolution of `MeanGlobalWealth`

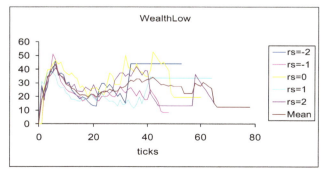

Figure 8: The evolution of `WealthLow`

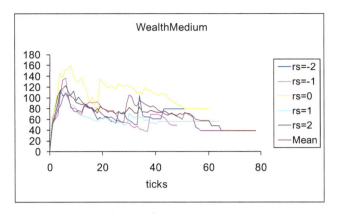

Figure 9: The evolution of `WealthMedium`

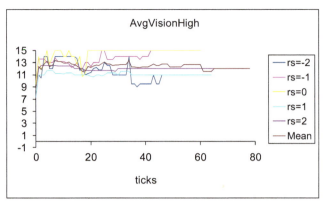

Figure 13: The evolution of `AvgVisionHigh`

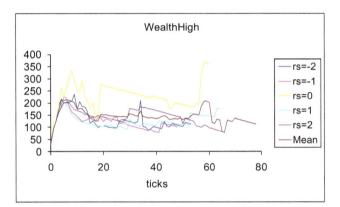

Figure 10: The evolution of `WealthHigh`

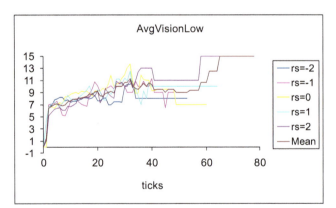

Figure 11: The evolution of `AvgVisionLow`

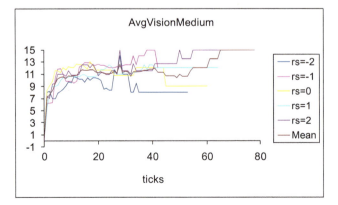

Figure 12: The evolution of `AvgVisionMedium`

INDEX

A

Agent-based Artificial Society, 3, 8, 9, 10
agent-based computational economics, 9
agent-based simulation, 3, 22
agents, 1, 3, 4, 5, 6, 8, 9, 12, 20, 22, 23, 24, 29, 32, 36
algorithms, 1, 2, 3, 4, 5, 6, 8, 9, 11, 12, 13, 15, 22, 25
An agent based model implementation, 22
analysis and modeling of experimental results, 43
Anthropology, 2, 19
Applied Computational Mathematics, 1, 2, 8, 9, 10
Artificial Social Group, 8, 9
artificial society, 1, 3, 8, 9, 10, 22

C

catastrophe theory, 8
chaos theory, 8
complex systems, 1, 3, 22, 43
Computational Biology, 1
Computational Chemistry, 1, 2
Computational Economics, 1, 2, 9
Computational Electrodynamics, 1, 2
computational experiment, 31, 43
Computational Finance, 1, 2
Computational Fluid Dynamics, 1, 2
Computational Geophysics, 1, 2
Computational Mechanics, 1, 2
Computational Physics, 1, 2
Computational statistics, 1, 2
computer experiments, 43, 44, 46, 48, 53
cross-disciplinary scientific research, 1

E

Economics, 1, 2, 8, 9, 20, 23
Education, 2, 20
equilibrium oriented approach, 8
evolutionary economics, 9
experimental planning, 43
experimentation phase, 43

G

Geography, 2, 20

H

heterogeneous social agents, 3
History, 2, 4, 20

I

in silico experiment, 43
intelligent agents, 1

L

Law, 1, 2, 20, 21, 55
linear models, 8

Linguistics, 2, 21

M
modeling phase, 43
Monte Carlo Methods, 3
multi agent-based computational model, 3
multi-agent social systems, 3

N
NetLogo, 1, 3, 4, 22, 23, 24, 25, 26, 27, 28, 31, 34, 44, 54
NetLogo platform, 1

P
parameters, 1, 3, 4, 5, 8, 9, 10, 11, 12, 13, 23, 24, 25, 29, 30, 41, 43, 44
Political Science, 2, 21
Psychology, 2, 21, 23

S
Social Sciences, 1, 2, 3, 4, 6, 8, 9, 19, 23
Social Work, 2, 21
Sociology, 2, 21
Study of multiple experiments, 43

T
theory of dissipative structures, 8

V
variables, 3, 4, 5, 6, 8, 9, 10, 11, 13, 17, 18, 23, 24, 25, 29, 30, 31, 37, 40, 43, 44, 48, 53

www.ingramcontent.com/pod-product-compliance
Lightning Source LLC
Chambersburg PA
CBHW041419050326
40689CB00002B/571